TESTIMONIALS

"Betty Galvano personifies the unique blend of talent, passion, faith and determination reflected in women lucky to live at the Rehearsal Club -- of course, she found the perfect Prince while living there! I'm grateful to call you my friend, Betty."

—Denise Pence, aka "Katie" (G L), RC Chair, 2015

"Betty Galvano has touched the hearts of so many over the past 20 years as a volunteer with Hope Hospice. Her willingness to sit at the bedside to comfort a patient or to help a grieving family has brought peace, dignity, and comfort to people in our care. She has also been an active member of our Honor Guard, paying tribute to veterans entering life's final chapter. It is a joy to know Betty and to experience her spirit as part of her circle of caring."

— Samira K. Beckwith, President/CEO, Hope HealthCare Services

"*Zapped by the Spirit* is the story of one woman's journey to find God and the Catholic Faith. It is a riveting reflection on the way that God works in our lives and how God is never separated from us. Betty conveys her deep personal relationship with God through stories of her childhood, her married years and what it is like to live the simple life, while being committed to doing the will of Jesus Christ. Betty wants to inspire people to seek out the love of God and for them to feel his love in their lives."

—Father Anthony R. Hewitt, JCL
Administrator St. Francis Xavier Parish,
Fort Myers, FL

"St. Paul tells us in Galatians 5:22 that two of the first fruits of the Holy Spirit in our lives are love and joy. These two gifts shine brightly in this book, as well as in the life of Betty Galvano who graciously and delightfully shares her profound Catholic journey to the Lord Jesus and His Church. Betty's life and journey was no stranger to the cross, but always blessed with love and joy. May all who read this life story of the operations and gifts of the Lord's grace in her life also be 'zapped by the Spirit'."

—Father Dennis J. Cooney
Pastor of St. Raphael's Parish
Lehigh Acres, Florida

"What an inspiration to read! A beautiful account of God at work in a very special lady."

—Reverend Monsignor Stephen E. McNamara
Church of the Resurrection of Our Lord
Fort Myers, Florida

"Betty Galvano's life story is not only miraculous and uplifting, it's entertaining and inspiring! Her story will make you laugh, reflect and believe more strongly in the presence and power of God. Betty has thankfully, written down all of her wonderful life stories and turned them into this book. I know it will surely bless and inspire countless people!"

—Former Miss Georgia USA 1990, Professional Model
Actress, Spokesperson and Catholic Speaker
Brenda Sharman

ZAPPED

BY THE

SPIRIT

ZAPPED

BY THE

SPIRIT

BETTY BIGGERS GALVANO

Zapped By The Spirit

Author Consultant: Felice Gerwitz of MediaAngels.com

Cover Illustration: MelindaMartin.me

Printed in the United States of America

A portion of the proceeds from this book will go charity.

This book is dedicated to the love of my life Phil,

my children:
Philip, Elizabeth, William, Richard, Peter, and Mary,

as well as my extended family;

and to those who pass on the Catholic faith.

ABOUT THE AUTHOR

Betty Biggers Galvano was one of the youngest members of the NY Academy of Sciences. As a microbiologist, she joined the Faculty of NYU's Washington Square School of Arts and Sciences. During this period, she founded a club for over sixty street children in Greenwich Village. Betty graduated from the Barbizon Modeling School and Carnegie Hall's TV Commercial School. She modeled at home and abroad, was introduced on *The Ed Sullivan Show* as one of the ten Top Ten Models in the USA and performed on stage with the famed Rockettes. She wrote for *Catholic Parent Magazine* for years and was a member of the Golf Writers of America. She became a widow in 1996 and moved to Ft. Myers to be with her daughter. She graduated from the Edmund B. Rice School of Theology & Ministry in 1997. She is a volunteer at St. Francis Xavier, a member of the Council of Catholic Women, advocate of Respect for Life, founder of St. Therese Prayer Garden, and more. Passing on her Catholic Faith is her passion. Betty married her soul mate, Phil Galvano ,and they were blessed with six children. They lived in New York and Florida.

Betty can be contacted at Betty@MediaAngels.com.

CONTENTS

PROLOGUE

I t is very easy for me to say that my mom, Betty Biggers Galvano, is the most incredible woman I know. It is hard not to say the most wonderful things about her. Throughout my life she has always been the perfect example of everything I need to be as a woman, and a person. I owe my life to her.

Without her faith and devotion to God, and her belief in life and miracles, I would not be here today. The year of 1973 was a year of devastation to many unborn children due to the case of Roe vs. Wade. Even my own life was at stake when the doctor thought it would be wise for my mother to abort me. But, thank God, my mother said no to him and yes to life no matter what the personal consequences. She believed God could do anything, and she still does. Here I am today a grown, healthy woman, a wife and mother, a professional singer (mainly for the Catholic Church) and an LPGA Golf Professional. Life has been brilliant for me, especially with the family I was given and the gifts of talent bestowed on me. Thank you, Mom for giving me a chance!

I am sure I speak for all of my siblings when I say how blessed we have been to have the parents we have. Mom's story will take you on the journey of the type of person that influenced our lives. Her story is an example of what a life looks like that is given totally over, in trust to God. St. Mother Theresa said, "Not all of us can do great things. But we can do small things with great love." This is how Mom lived her life, although, she continuously fell into doing great things through the workings of the Holy Spirit.

Betty Biggers Galvano is a woman of courage, beauty, intelligence, love, and never ending joy. She is a teacher of life and how to truly live out the Catholic Faith in all aspects of life. Her story is exciting! It is a story of tender romance and glamour, and charisma, yet it tells of a woman that loves simplicity. Her life is always based on putting God and other's needs first. Even today she does not stop giving of herself in the service of others. Most of all, Mom has this incredible spirituality. It overwhelms others who are around her. I am sure you will soon learn this.

I was blessed being the youngest of six because after everyone moved out it was just Dad, Mom and I. Dad was continuously teaching me skills of all kinds and sharing his wisdom, and Mom and I grew close together spiritually. My parents traveled on the professional golf tour with me. We have many diverse memories such as the time we were in Louisiana, and ate a bucket-full of crayfish in our hotel room and the time we stopped at EWTN to see a viewing of *Mother Angelica Live*. After Dad passed away my mother and I moved into a house we bought in Ft. Myers, Florida. She was the best roommate a girl could have! Her meals were certainly the best in town. We grew extremely close. Sometimes I think our closeness caused us to "zap" each other with spirit. Our time together is something I will always treasure because this is when I became truly devout in the One True Church. We both were constantly doing vocational work at St. Francis Xavier and we shared pilgrimages together, one in particular changed me forever.

Our family was blessed to share our lives with this amazing woman. We have much in which to be thankful and we owe so much to our mom. Thank you, Mom, for being our wonderful, beautiful mom. We love you! I love you!

Mary Galvano-Bajohr

THUNDER AND LIGHTNING

Thunder roared, lightning lit up the sky, and windows rattled, as the lights flickered in the maternity ward of the Georgia Baptist Hospital, in downtown Atlanta. My mother let out one last scream and a faint cry of a newborn baby alerted all within hearing distance that I had arrived on August 6, 1935. In her exhaustion, Mother heard the doctor say it was a girl, she smiled faintly. How happy my father would be, she thought. They already had a two-year old boy, my brother, Fred. My parents were hoping for a girl.

A nurse took me to be cleaned up, weighed and measured, even before Mother had a chance to see me. Mother waited for the nurse to place me in her arms. After what seemed like an eternity, the doctor was back at my mother's bedside without a baby. His face was grim, as he shared the unhappy news. A Baptist Minister was immediately summoned to baptize me.

The doctor said I weighed in at four pounds, with a skull that was a thin membrane, without bone. And, I was a "blue baby," with lungs not opening properly and poor blood circulation. The doctor and his staff gave no hope for my survival, and predicted I would not leave the hospital.

I was put into an incubator, which a nurse rolled into my mother's room next to her bedside. As Mother took her first look at me, her heart sank. But, there was hope. She knew there was someone who could change anything and she called out to God to spare me. She prayed with all her might. Mother was a prayer warrior, she never lost hope and she trusted God for a miracle.

Against all odds, two weeks later my parents took me home. The doctor still had little hope for my survival. Even if by some miracle I lasted for some time, he had said that there was no way I could live more than five years. My circulation and breathing would always be poor. I had developed intolerance for milk, even breast milk. Coca-Cola Syrup was the only thing my digestive system would tolerate for the next three months.

Two days after I arrived home, once again a fierce thunderstorm lit up the sky and thunder rocked the little white frame house my parents called home. Then, a brilliant flash of light illuminated the house as lightning struck an electrical power cable that led into the house. The cable snapped and now was whipping back and forth across the eight steps leading up to the front door. Inside the house streaks of electricity shot from doorknob to doorknob and other metal objects. Mother was frightened as she feared we would be electrocuted if we remained in the house.

Praying with all her might again, Mother wrapped me in a rubber raincoat. Cautiously, she pushed open the screen door with a wooden broomstick. Holding me close, she carefully inched her way across the porch, as flashes of electricity spewed out from the downed cable. When she reached the banister on the far side of the porch, she held me tight and jumped over the banister landing into bushes. Five hours later that is where workmen from the Georgia Power Company found us.

Five months later, I was rushed back to the hospital. Mother noticed I was hardly breathing and I was turning blue. One of my lungs had collapsed, and I was in a coma. The doctor left the examining table saying there was nothing more anyone could do, and I would be dead within two hours.

Mother stood at the window in my room on the second floor of the hospital. Rumblings of thunder broke the silence as heavy raindrops splashed across the windowpane, mirroring her turmoil, and matching tears rolled down her cheeks. Suddenly, a brilliant ball of light lit up on the lawn below. As Mother watched, it slowly rose up to the window where Mother, startled, stood back in disbelief. It floated through the window, across the room and came to rest for a few seconds over my frail little body. It then disappeared back through the window just as it had come.

My mother didn't realize a nurse had come into the room, and she too witnessed the ball of light. Mother and the nurse exchanged looks and stood rooted in place, afraid to move until a faint cry alerted them that my coma had broken. The nurse ran down the hallway shouting, "Miracle! Miracle!"

Within minutes, the doctor and nurses flocked into the room to see for themselves that indeed a miracle had taken place, as I was moving and making noises. The miracle is attributed to answered prayers, but my mother was not the only one praying. The congregation of the little Baptist Church where we attended, gathered together in the church that afternoon to intercede.

Years later I would learn through Lightning Strike International that lightning sometimes appears as balls of light. Ball lightning has been mistaken for UFOs, as they bounce across hills in the Midwest. Once a nun told me of an experience she had with ball lightning. She was sweeping the floor of an upstairs bedroom in a convent, where there was a row of beds. All of a sudden a loud clap of thunder startled her half to death, as three balls of light came in from an opened window and rolled under a bed. After a few minutes she cautiously pulled up the covers and peered under the bed. There was nothing there!

In 1938 when I was three years old, I moved with my family to Avondale, a suburb of Atlanta. We would always remember this home as the "Little Green House", since it was painted a dark evergreen. Our family now included my sister, Dot, who was two years younger than me. Daddy had graduated from Georgia Tech

University. Avondale was nearer to the Chemical Company where he worked as a textile chemist.

Daddy and Mother knew the fresh country air would be good for my health. My mother guarded me like a hawk, ever since the doctor had warned her, at my birth that it would be a miracle if I lived. To strengthen my lungs, Mother had me lie on the floor before bedtime every night and breathe deeply with a heavy Encyclopedia on top of my stomach. She told me to see how high I could make it go. She knew spending time outdoors; gardening, raising chickens and even having fresh milk from our two cows would be good for me. In the silence of the night, millions of stars lit up the dark sky filling us with wonder and awe for God's creation. It was a big contrast to bright lights, blinking signs, honking cars and sirens we had been accustomed to in downtown Atlanta.

Mother planted flowers everywhere. A small bridge covered with pink Dorothy Perkins Roses led over a bubbling brook to the front door. Mother would say we are all flowers in God's garden. It would be boring if we were all roses, daises or the same type. We are unique and beautiful, created in His own design. Years later I would learn Mother was quoting St. Therese, the Little Flower.

Dot, Fred and I played with minnows and tadpoles that swam in the creek. Sometimes we chased ducks and chickens around the yard. Our Chow Dogs, Chow Mein and Chop Suey, guarded us wherever we went. Much to our dismay, they always barked whenever they thought Mother should check on us.

I'll never forget the day Chow Mein chased a mouse through the house. He chased the mouse right into the bathroom where Daddy was sitting on the toilet and reading the newspaper. The mouse ran up Daddy's pant leg. The next thing I knew, Daddy was jumping up and down and hollering for me to go away.

One night when we came home after visiting my grandparents, a torrential rain was bursting from the sky. Daddy pulled his Model T Ford as close as he could to the little bridge, then we all ran as fast as we could across it, and into the house. We still got soaked. We heard moaning and groaning from outside, behind the kitchen where January and February, our two cows desperately needed to be milked! Daddy had no choice. However he came up with a brilliant idea, at least he thought so. He took two blankets, a flashlight, a milk stool, and grabbed the milk pails, as he went out the back door. He splashed through rivers of red mud running through the backyard to the pasture.

Daddy led the cows up near the house. Now he threw the blankets over the double clotheslines making a tent. Next he put the stool and milk pails under the blankets. Then he tugged and pulled the bewildered cows under the blankets. Mother, Fred and I watched in amazement from a window. In the beginning the milking went well until Chow Mein and Chop Suey sneaked out the door, and were howling under the blankets. They spooked the cows who kicked over the buckets of milk. The clothesline snapped causing Daddy and the cows to become tangled in the blankets. Mother ran to the rescue, slipped in the mud and fell on top of Daddy. January and February struggled to their feet and ran back to the pasture. The dogs ran back into the house tracking mud everywhere. Daddy and Mother, covered with mud and milk sat there laughing in the rain. At least the cows had been milked and were out of their misery.

One morning I woke up sneezing with a barking cough. I knew Mother was concerned because she kept taking my temperature. She gave me hot kettle tea with honey to drink. She covered my chest with Vicks Vapor Rub and made me stay under the covers. By afternoon it was difficult for me to breathe. My fever was now 106 degrees! When the doctor arrived, I was already in a coma; only a faint heartbeat remained in my limp, little body. My breathing had nearly stopped. After the doctor examined me, he shook his head and said I was dying. I would not last the hour. He reminded Mother he predicted from the beginning I would not live beyond five years. The doctor left for another emergency, saying he would return later to sign the death certificate.

My parents, grandparents and a minister, all with heavy hearts shed tears, as they stood around my little iron bed. In sadness they joined in prayer. The Methodist Minister from my family's new church gave me my second baptism. Suddenly, a crash of thunder shook the house. Hail and heavy rain pelted the tin roof as lightning streaked across the sky, and the wind howled. The lights flickered throughout the house. Again the prayers of my loved ones reached up to the Gates of Heaven.

Suddenly, the storm stopped. A large ray of sunshine came through the window, and across my bed engulfing me in golden light. I suddenly opened my eyes, sat up and pointed towards the window. "Look at the beautiful lady with wings! She is holding hands with children! They are dancing around the tree!"

Then I fell back down on my pillow. I was no longer in a coma. The storm continued to rage, once again. Everyone witnessed the storm stop, and the ray of golden light engulfing my frail body, as I lay in my bed. They saw wet leaves of the huge maple tree glistening in the sunlight. However, no one except me had seen the beautiful lady with feathery wings with her flowing pink and light green gown and her long blond hair dancing about her. No one had seen the children. But I knew I had seen them, because I counted all six of them, and I have never forgotten the incident. The children were so happy, so full of joy and laughter, that I had wanted to join them.

Someone once asked me if I thought the children might have been the six children I would eventually have as a mother and that the tree represented the Tree of Life. I cannot answer that, and neither could the doctor who returned to my bedside that night answer why I was still alive after he predicted, three times, that I was actively dying. No one could explain why there was always thunder and lightning when I received new life.

I truly believe prayers brought the healings. God hears all prayers, especially prayers from mothers for their children. I believe prayer is the strongest force in the universe. As hard as it is for some of you to believe, for me it is obvious that God sends His angels as protection, and has entrusted us especially to our guardian angel who is always near.

In my heart and soul, I thank our Heavenly Father for sending angels to watch over me as well as you. Thank you, God, for creating angels! In the Bible this verse stands out for me: "For to his angels he has given command about you, that they guard you in all your ways." (Psalms 91: 11).

If you don't believe there is such a thing as a Guardian Angel, I urge you to pray to the Lord, and ask Him about the phenomenon of angels. This may seem like a foreign concept to you. In prayer the Lord can help you understand and bring things to mind that will help you to see the amazing purpose of angels in our lives. If you have never spoken with your Guardian Angel I encourage you to try. In the Catholic Catechism of the Catholic Church: 328, it says, "The existence of the spiritual, non-corporeal beings that Sacred Scripture usually calls 'angels' is a truth of faith. The witness of Scripture is as clear as the unanimity of Tradition."

THE HOUSE IN THE STICKS

ife continued in another direction when in 1940 my father took a job as a textile chemist in Spartenburg, South Carolina. We moved to a house in the country with a promise of electricity and phone lines that would eventually reach out to the countryside. The white two story turn-of-the-century house sat in the middle of thirty acres of red dirt, plowed neatly and mostly planted with corn. The house was elevated on columns of flat rocks taken from a nearby river.

In the meantime, gathering firewood from the nearby woods, to stoke the fire in the old iron stove in the kitchen for Mother to cook was routine. When the weather inevitably turned cold, my father built a fire in the old potbelly stove or in the fireplace in the kitchen to heat our home. Two red dusty paths led away from the back porch. One led to a well where we lowered a bucket on a rope and pulled up sparkling cool water. The other led to the outhouse where an old Sears and Roebuck Catalog hung on a rope and corncob husks were piled in the corner for convenience. At night when it was dark or the weather was inclement, we used slop jars that were kept under our beds. Invariably, one of us would knock it over. What a mess and what an odor!

A long flat plank stretched across the back porch. A mirror hung from a nail for my father to shave. A basin of water rested on the plank for washing up. In the evenings Mother heated a kettle of water on the old iron stove and poured it into a galvanized tin tub. Quickly, my sister, our two brothers and I took turns jumping in and out for a quick bath. Then, we donned long johns with "snapping doors" in the back just in case we had to make a quick visit to the slop jar. Then we were led off to bed, as Mother held a lighted candle up the stairs to illuminate the way.

At night a kerosene lamp in the kitchen gave the only light in the dark house, but outside millions and trillions of stars and the moon often lit up the night sky. Many nights our little family sat on the back porch searching for shooting stars. My mother was fond of saying, "Famous people are like shooting stars dazzling others with their light, but common people are like the other stars that shine forever and ever." Later I would recall these words with fondness.

At four, I imagined I saw the face of the "man in the moon" and this really intrigued me. I still look for his smile in a full moon, and I have never been disappointed. I was very naïve and it took me a long time to realize that a "cow did not jump over the moon" as I learned in the Mother Goose rhyme.

Once a week an ice truck stopped at the house and a bowlegged old man in coveralls emerged. Using big iron tongs that swayed side-to-side, he carried a huge block of ice into the kitchen, for our icebox, to keep our milk, butter and cheese cool. By the end of the week if there was enough ice left, my father chipped it up with an ice pick. He then layered the wooden ice cream maker with ice and salt. We all took turns cranking the handle, so that the cylinder in the middle filled with milk and fresh fruit churned, round and round. Mother's special recipe produced the best ice cream in the world, a special treat on Sunday.

The farmer who tended our corn fields lived down the red dirt road and arrived accompanied with his stubborn mule, to plow the large area near the house. Sometimes he let me hold onto the handles of the plow. He yelled "Gittee up!" Away we went stepping through soft red mud, as he plowed the ground. Sometimes mud oozed between the toes of my little bare feet.

Our garden was huge. There were no insecticides back then, so Mother gave my sister, Dot, and me the job of walking up and down the rows and rows of beans, tomatoes, peppers and other vegetables to pick off bugs or worms and their eggs and drop them into a small jar that contained a little bit of kerosene to kill them. During harvest time, Mother canned all the vegetables.

We didn't have electricity, or a washing machine and washing clothing required fetching water from the well. But, there was another option. A little-middle-aged woman lived in a small cottage at the end of our field and took in laundry to wash. Mother brought her our dirty laundry, which she washed in a big black kettle of water that had been heated over a fire in the yard. After the items had hung on an outside line to dry, I used to sit in her kitchen and watch her iron. Linen, cotton, silk and wool were the only fabrics available then; nylon, rayon and permanent-press fabrics were not yet on the market. Everything had to be ironed. She had two irons that were heated on a potbelly stove. She used one at a time, as she ironed. When the one she was using got cold, she switched to the other.

During harvest time our home was a very busy place as neighbors, women and their children, came from the countryside to our house through various modes of transportation. Some walked; others rode up on a horse. The women sat together on our large back porch, shucking corn, snapping beans and shelling peas. Once harvesting and canning season ended, they got together to sew, embroider or braid rugs from old clothing. The women had fun sharing stories and enjoyed news that came from the men who worked in town. This was the only way the news traveled since radios needed electricity which was lacking in the country.

The children had fun, as well. Sometimes we took turns riding one of the horses or searching for turtles in ditches alongside the dirt road. Sometimes the girls laid out the perimeter of a house with sticks or stones in the yard and played "house". We made dolls out of discarded corncobs. Corn silk made beautiful hair for our dolls. We chased butterflies, gathered wildflowers and made daisy chains out of clover, which we adorned upon ourselves and pretended to be princesses.

Sometimes, the boys galloped about the fields on make-believe horses pretending to be cowboys. I felt sorry for the chickens that ran for their lives from their pretend lassos. Games such as hide-and-seek, kick the can, jump rope and marbles added to the fun for the boys and girls alike.

One summer day when our mothers were sitting on the porch, they noticed a strange hound dog slowly walking through the field near the house. Suddenly, pandemonium erupted as a myriad of voices began screaming at the children, "Mad dog! Mad dog!" Fortunately, everyone scurried up the steps and into the kitchen before the dog, foaming from his mouth, reached the porch. The rabid dog then disappeared under the house and into the crawl space.

We waited inside the house for several more hours for my father to come home. We did not dare go outside. As soon as we heard the motor of his car coming up the long driveway, my mother screamed to him from the porch about the mad dog under the house. His car windows were down since it was a hot summer day, and cars did not have air conditioning. My father heard her and pulled his car up against the back porch steps. Mother handed him his shotgun and bullets. He then, drove back a little way from the house. Cautiously, he got out of the car, loaded the gun, stooped down and tried to find the dog. It was not long before the dog came out. While everyone in the house was praying, Daddy aimed and pulled the trigger of his shotgun. The dog keeled over in the dirt. Foam still leaked from his mouth. Daddy was everybody's hero! Later the dog was buried, far away from the house.

Our mothers took us berry picking when they were in season. We each carried our own little pail and picked the sweetest and tastiest blackberries and strawberries in the world. Sometimes we ended up eating more than we took home. Mother did not mind, as she always seemed to have plenty of fruit to make her delicious pies.

Sometimes we waded in a creek with the other mothers and children searching for clay. When we found it, we scooped out lumps of soft red clay from the creek bank and took buckets of it back to the house. We spent endless hours creating all kinds of sculptures. Sometimes we decorated our masterpieces with acorns and pebbles, let them dry and painted them to give away for presents.

On Saturday mornings our family put on bathing suits and hiked through the woods at the edge of the property, to the small river rolling down over huge boulders. The water fell into a pond near an old watermill. The huge wheel, inside the mill, turned round and round through the splashing water, grinding corn into cornmeal or grits on huge stones.

Other families joined us at the top of the boulders. We took turns sitting in the rushing water and sliding down the boulders creating a big splash into the pond below. Daddy always held me tight on his lap, as we slid down the boulders into the pond. This was our very own water park!

Mother often took Dot and me on walks through the woods. She taught us nature is God's greatest cathedral. We searched for wildflowers and delighted when we found violets, Johnny-in-the pulpits, and sweet buds which we picked and took home to make sachets. We placed these in our drawers with our clothes, to give them a sweet fragrance. We often sat quietly on soft green moss, and listened in silence for God's voice. He always spoke to me, sometimes in a radiant sunbeam, spreading light through the trees in the dark woods. Other times His voice came through birds flying about singing songs of joy. Mother said birds sing only for the glory of God.

This "house in the sticks" was not only a magical place for me, but a soulful place to grow up. Our imaginations had no limits. Dot and I searched for Thumbelina, Tom Thumb and other fairies in pink and yellow hollyhocks, daises and other flowers. Sometimes we imagined seeing fairies glide by on the backs of butterflies and dragonflies. But at the end of our playing, we sat down in the grass and sang praises of thanks to God for His flowers, creatures and the beauty of nature all around us.

It was a sad and tearful day when we were forced to pack-up and move back into the city. It was 1941 and with the rumors of war, the city officials decided to indefinitely postpone installing electricity, phone lines or paving the road to our home. If there was a war, we needed to be where we could have better communication with others. And so this phase of my young life came to an end, but it was never forgotten.

WORLD WAR II

As the ear piercing sirens blasted throughout the usually calm and quiet neighborhood, my mother and father raced down the hallway, past the living room and burst out the front door. Curiously, I left my "make-believe house" under an end table in the living room. I picked up my Sonya Heine Doll, my constant companion, and helped her glide to the front door on her tiny ice skates.

Neighbors and many other people crowded the street. Not everyone had a radio the only means for getting the latest up-to-date, news. Just then a city official slowly drove a pickup truck down the street. As he passed by, he repeatedly shouted through a megaphone, "Japs bomb Pearl Harbor!" At the news, people screamed and many cried out with fear and anxiety. Some called out to God to save our families and country. It was December 7, 1941, a day that I would never forget. Neither would anyone else who lived in our country during that time!

Three days later there was a repeat of the event, this time the man with the megaphone driving the pickup truck passed slowly down the streets throughout town with this news, "War declared!" World War II had indeed been declared by President, Franklin Delano Roosevelt. Not since the American Revolution or World

War I would patriotism peak so high, as people of the United States of America vowed to defend our country. The motto, "One nation under God, indivisible, with liberty and justice for all," sang in the hearts of many. At only six-years old I didn't understand the extent of what the coming weeks would bring to me and my family. Nor did I realize anything would ever be the same again. The world turned upside down.

Women joined the Red Cross in droves. Every afternoon after school, they met in neighborhood homes to make bandages needed in the many hospitals springing up in war zones. Navy blue veils with white bands and a bright red cross covered their heads. While the women made bandages, school children were taken to a roped off, designated street patrolled by other mothers. Truthfully, the children loved it since the activities consisted of: skating, riding scooters, jump roping, playing tag, hop scotching and marbles. Those who had homework sat on the curb until finished then joined in the fun.

At school our Stars-and-Stripes flew high, as everyone proudly recited the *Pledge of Allegiance*. When the music teacher struck the first chord of the Star Spangled Banner on the piano in the auditorium, everyone jumped to attention. My dance class featured routines to *Anchors Aweigh, This is the Army Mister Jones, Over There!* and other patriotic songs.

When my brother, Fred, sister Dot and I came down with measles, Mother put our beds in one room where we could keep warm by the fireplace, and she could monitor our fevers and red spots that developed into oozing boils. A young nurse from the County Health Office came to check on us, and Mother asked her if she had heard the new song by Irving Berlin that Kate Smith was singing. She had, and she stood at attention and reverently sang, *God Bless America,* I can recall that moment, vividly. That song later became the theme song for our nation.

While patriotism ran high, so did tensions, as more and more men were drafted, or voluntarily signed up to join the military. On the home front, women were needed to help fill vacant jobs. Entire high school graduating classes left immediately for armed service after receiving their diplomas. Current news was still dependent upon people with radios, who shared whatever they heard of relevance with their neighbors.

How I longed to be back at the "house in the sticks" where everything was peaceful, stars lit up the evening sky, crickets chirped and birds sang for the glory of God. It was not to be, as the transition of moving back into town became harder with the news that "Uncle Sam" drafted my father to make disinfectants and soaps for the military. We immediately moved to Conover, North Carolina, where my father operated a small plant, the Habow Chemical Company. Mother was needed to help my father make soaps. My brother, sister, and I were needed to sift sawdust that was used to make a sweeping compound to sanitize hallways in hospitals and schools.

If we did not grow it, we did not eat it! Every class at school was required to plant a ten-foot by twelve-foot vegetable garden on the far end of the playground. Students tended the "Victory Gardens" at recess before they could play. Knowing how to produce one's own food was important. Most students tended home gardens after school and cared for chickens raised for meat and eggs. Cows had to be milked, and I sometimes milked our goats, since my sister was allergic to cow's milk.

We raised rabbits for food, but we also, raised and took care of five hundred white angora rabbits for the U.S. Army. Fur was gently pulled from the rabbits before it became matted and dirty, then the fur was sent off in large tin cans to make warm sweaters or coats for the Army. The rabbits were not harmed.

During cotton-picking time, farmers brought buckboard wagons that were covered with hay and pulled by horses to the school. After dismissal those with permission, jumped onto the wagons and rode out into the country to pick cotton. We were each given a big burlap sack, and received ten cents for every bag we filled.

Conover was a very small town where most everyone worked in either the glove mill, or the hosiery mill. There were only two churches, a Dutch Reformed and a Missouri Lutheran. Although there was an elementary school, students had to ride a bus three miles away to attend Newton-Conover High School. The town sported a movie house, two drug stores and a furniture store on Main Street. That's it!

Our two-story home sat on a hill, bordered by the playground of the elementary school. Our home became Headquarters of the Senior Girl Scouts, known as the Mariners. The high school aged girls wore navy blue uniforms, black ties and sailor hats. Mother was well trained, and she even knew Juliet Lowe, Founder of the Girl Scouts, in her own early scouting days. The Red Cross helped train the girls in taking care of young children and babies, as well as First Aid. We learned survival skills from the U.S. Coast Guard, along with my mother, who trained the girls to evacuate our town, lead women and children into the woods on the mountainside and survive on whatever vegetation they might find. We learned to make trails and then, cover them up for safety. Silence was the key to survival because our voices echoed in the mountains. Sometimes we slept in blankets on the forest floor, and boiled water from a lake or brook to drink. We learned to make a fire by rubbing stones together for sparks over dry leaves, and then that the fire should be extinguished as soon as possible to avoid detection.

Many other mothers helped teach the Mariners skills, such as: canning vegetables from the gardens, and preserving local fruit. My mother made the tastiest apple butter, a favorite of all. Everyone shared whatever they had, especially with those who were not able to produce their own food.

The Mariner Scouts ran the Canteen at our house every Saturday night to welcome service boys home on furloughs. Usually refreshments consisted of water and fruit, if available, since sugar, butter, meat, sodas, coffee and many other items were rationed. Dot and I dangled our legs through the upstairs banister and watched and listened as popular tunes played on our Victrola. The Mariner Girl Scouts and young men danced the jitter-bug or shag to tunes of Glenn Miller or *Dipsey Doodle, Hubba, Hubba, Hubba* and others.

Frequently, air raids came followed by huge roaring bombers overhead, shaking our homes to the very foundation. Homework often had to be completed in a closet with a flashlight during blackouts. Convoys of tanks, jeeps, and trucks were frightening to watch, as they roared through town. It was common for the young and old alike to stand at attention and salute the convoys or formations of military aircraft flying overhead. We never knew if an attack was imminent.

Worst were the reports of loved ones killed or missing in action. My heart nearly broke when one of my best friends said her brother had been shot by the enemy, as he was parachuting out of his burning plane. Tear streaked faces were common wherever one went, as everyone had loved ones involved in the war. This was a sad but special time for our nation because everyone really loved and cared for each another—in experiencing the war together there was a profound sense of unity.

I cried myself to sleep almost every night, as I wondered, *Why did God make us, if we were just going to die? Didn't God love us?* I shared these thoughts with my mother.

She consoled me, "God loves us very much. Have faith and hope in Him. See God in everything. See His face in everyone." Then, she told me to be like Pollyanna, who was a favorite character in a book I enjoyed. She encouraged me to always find a reason to be glad. Mother also said, "Smile and the world smiles with you. Weep and you weep alone, and a smile is such a little thing, but oh what joy it brings! A heart in grief and great sorrow is soon relieved from that sad state." Through the years I have found my mother's words of wisdom to be true, and I grew up joyful, smiling and still smile much of the time!

Early one morning in August after we had fed the chickens and gathered the eggs, I drove into downtown Atlanta with my grandmother. I always spent my summers with her. At the office where she worked, Grandmother suddenly stopped typing, jumped up from her desk, and grabbed my hand urgently, "Let's get out of here! We need to get home!"

We hadn't gotten very far down to the street, when we witnessed all of Atlanta going wild! Sirens, horns blasting, people shouting and dancing in the streets and papers thrown from skyscrapers peppered the sky.

World War II was over! We learned the atomic bomb had been dropped on Hiroshima!

This was another day no one in our country, especially those who lived at the time would soon forget. We learned the troops were coming home, and finally we could think about something else, besides war! I would never forget this day for other reasons, since August 6th, 1945 was my tenth birthday. For the rest of my life, I would never be able to celebrate my birthday without thinking of those who perished that day that others might live. As I reflect on that time I remember another, Jesus, my Love, who also died, unselfishly for others. I am comforted because I know those who love Him and keep His ways will live with Him forever.

SURVIVING A SUMMER OF DREAD

The bell rang as the doors of the old, two-story, yellow brick schoolhouse burst open. I raced out with the other children, screaming and laughing into the late May sunshine. Summer vacation! Freedom! This summer would be more than an escape from arithmetic and homework. It would be the first summer vacation my friends and I could remember that wasn't dominated by the fears and horror of World War II. It was 1946, and the war was over. My friends and I in Conover, North Carolina had plans for every moment.

My sister Dot and our friends couldn't wait to play dress-up in our mothers' discarded clothes, which we kept crammed in an old suitcase. We would play with paper dolls that we kept neatly filed in old magazines. Our mud pies would be unsurpassed. We planned to: splash in the old swimming hole, play kick–the-can with neighborhood kids, picnic in fields of daises, brown-eyed-Susans, and clover, which we would then weave into crowns and necklaces to wear, while dancing and singing though the meadows.

Every year, the children on our street worked all summer on a stage show we acted, produced and directed. The stage was someone's porch and the parents all purchased tickets for five-cents. We knew this summer's show would be the best, since the war was over, and it was now easier to laugh and have fun.

But suddenly, in the middle of June, events took a turn for the worse.

One night, Dad came home from work and hardly said hello before he took mother aside into the parlor. He was not smiling, and when they came out, Mother's eyes were filled with tears. They asked us all to sit down in the living room. Dot, my two brothers Fred and Bill, and I filed in then waited, wide-eyed.

"I have some very bad news," Dad said in a low, soft voice. "A few weeks ago, someone in Conover became very ill. Two days later, he died. Since then, many more people in our area have contracted the disease, and more have died."

"It's polio," Mother said.

"Will we get polio and die, too?" asked Dot.

"If we get it, we don't have to die," I said. I was thinking of the president, Franklin Delano Roosevelt, who had survived polio but lived in a wheel chair until his death the year before. Miss Moore, my fourth-grade teacher, had made sure the class knew all about his strength and courage to overcome his afflictions and become president. He was our hero in a personal way.

"Everyone is being quarantined," Dad finally said.

"What does that mean?" we asked in unison.

"No one in Catawba County or this part of North Carolina is allowed to leave their yards unless it's for an essential job. Doctors can make house calls, but everyone else will have to stay home."

That was the final blow to our summer plans. Dad was allowed to keep working at the chemical company, especially since his expertise in making soap and disinfectants for the Army, during the war would now come in handy as the Red Cross and hospitals would need these products, desperately. However, he had to run the small plant by himself since his four employees were not allowed to leave their homes.

Conover became a ghost town. The post office, two pharmacies and a couple of gas stations were all that remained open.

Playgrounds were empty. Churches were silent. Fear, anxiety and gloom again ruled our hearts, just as they had during the war. Only this was worse if that was even possible, since the victims were our neighbors, our friends and relatives in our small community. I don't know what I would have done without Dot, two years younger, but a great friend and playmate.

Not everyone in town had a phone, but those that did called each other since it was our only means to stay in touch. The operator would say, "Number, please?" Sometimes the operator would connect several party lines and we could talk with all our friends at the same time. Other times we stood at the edge of our yards, waved and yelled back and forth. This became a daily ritual to assure each other of everyone's health. It was reassuring to know about those spared of the dreaded disease.

Then one day, Dot's classmates, the Kaiser twins, Keith and Kermit, didn't come out of their house. Dad broke the news to us that one of them had died of polio, the next day, the other died.

Dot and I cried for days. We could no longer stand at the edge of the yard and shout to our friends. We couldn't bear to look at the Kaiser house, and we were especially scared just like everyone else. We prayed for each other, we prayed for our friends, neighbors and even prayed for the animals, the dogs, cats, cows and chickens. We even prayed that our dolls wouldn't catch polio.

Every day the number of casualties grew. The Red Cross begged for volunteers at the makeshift hospitals where they set up huge tents in open fields. There was one nearby, just off the highway between Conover and Hickory. But, people were afraid to help. Mother had been a member of the Red Cross during the war and wanted to help, but she wasn't allowed to help because she had children at home. When Dad arrived home from work, he wouldn't let us hug him until he washed up.

Once Dot and I both came down with high fevers, and we threw up all night. Fred and Bill were forbidden to enter our room. Mother called the doctor, and he told her what to look for in case it was polio. He didn't want to come to the house unless he had to come. There was nothing he could do anyway but give us pain relievers. Mother sat in a small rocker at the foot of our twin beds all night. Now and then when I opened my eyes, I could see her lips moving. I knew she was praying. "God has everything under control," she would say.

By morning our fevers were gone, and later when Mother caught Dot and I catapulting Jell-O from our lunch trays at each other with our spoons, she didn't even scold us. She was so happy we were well.

Then one night in early June, after we had gone to sleep, Mother and Dad came into our bedrooms and woke us up. Using flashlights, they helped us put on our shoes and led us down the back stairs through the kitchen and across the back porch. We got into the family Plymouth parked in the driveway. We were too sleepy and dumbfounded to make much noise. Dad started the engine but didn't turn on the headlights. The car inched down our street, on down Main Street and out onto a country road, where Dad finally turned on the lights.

Mother and Dad wouldn't tell us where we were going. Soon, we fell asleep, but in my drowsiness, I heard my mother let out a big sigh, saying, "We're over the South Carolina border," and awhile later, "We're over the Georgia border." We were escaping the epidemic.

Around 6:00 a.m. we all knew we were in Atlanta, and Dad was turning the car into my grandmother's driveway. Dad had driven us over back roads all night to reach our destination, 187 miles from home. Mother and Dad had been afraid that if the car was stopped, we might give away the fact that we were leaving a quarantined area.

The next morning Mother and Dad left us with our grandparents and drove back to Conover. Mother was now free to volunteer at the Red Cross which was desperate for help. She spent hours, gently rubbing pain-racked bodies, changing bed linens and assisting the doctors and nurses. Mother was especially good at cheering people up, and telling stories. By the end of the summer, the quarantine was lifted, and we were reunited with our family finally able to return home.

The next spring, a major charitable organization held an event. Our teachers chaperoned us into town to see the lady in an iron lung, displayed in a furniture store window. Only her head stuck out of the long, silver cylinder attached to a table with wheels. She lay on her back, and we looked through small windows on the iron lung to see her chest gently rising and falling. Near her head was an air bag that breathed in and out along with her, the lady had beautiful blond curls, blue eyes and a smile I still remember. She was paralyzed from the neck down from polio, and it was feared she would have to live like that for the rest of her life. She couldn't even use a wheelchair. Her cheerfulness in answering our questions touched our hearts, and we worked harder than ever to collect dimes for a cure.

It would be years before the scourge of polio was eradicated from our community and others throughout the nation. From 1942 through 1947, according to history books, there was an average of 17,000 cases a year. Our part of North Carolina was among the hardest-hit areas. Then the number of cases doubled to 34,000 a year through 1951, and then an amazing 60,000 in 1952. It wasn't until 1953, that Jonas Salk invented his vaccine, and mass vaccinations were introduced in 1955. By 1989, there were only five cases of polio throughout the United States.

Still, the epidemic left many of our friends wearing braces, using crutches and wheelchairs, not to mention all those we knew who died. Perhaps in a small way, living through the perils of World War II had helped our community find the courage, hope and faith to help one another through the polio crisis. The song, *Dear Hearts and Gentle People*, popular during that time, could very easily have been written about my home town of Conover. Growing up during the polio epidemic taught me that life is precious and it increased the sympathy and love we had for each other, something I carry with me to this day.

CONVERSION

sank to my knees as dust filled the muggy moist air. The sounds of horse's hooves pounded the hard ground! Wails and cries of sorrow echoed from the crowds as thunder and huge cracks of lightning came from clouds above. *Was I imagining this?* It all seemed so real. Looking up, the eyes of the "dead Man" met mine. He was alive to me.

"We have to go! Get up!" Emily begged, as she tugged at my arm.

Sobbing, I cried out, "Let me stay! Please let me stay! Who is he? Who is the Man on the cross?"

Gradually, I got up from my knees, sobbing as I allowed Emily to lead me out. Ever so slowly, we walked down the aisle toward the rear door of the Sacred Heart Church in Atlanta. As I left the church, I glanced back once more, still sobbing as my heart broke. I was leaving the Man on the cross behind.

"Who is he?" I begged to know. "The Man on the cross is alive! He has stolen my heart! Emily, who is He?" I pleaded with her to tell me.

I was a nurses' aide at St. Joseph's Infirmary, a summer job I had just started in downtown Atlanta. It was the best paying job I could find. There had been no jobs in the small town of Conover, North

Carolina where I lived with my parents, brothers and sisters—after the polio epidemic my mother had another daughter, June.

My grandmother agreed that I could stay with her in Atlanta and find work. After all, I had spent nearly every summer of my life with Grandmother since I was three years old, just the two of us. I learned so much from her, and I gave her comfort in her loneliness.

I was sixteen, now and had one more year before graduating from high school. I was accepted at New York University's Washington Square School of Arts and Sciences. I needed to earn money to get there, once in New York I knew I could find a job to work my way through the university.

That evening I could hardly wait until after supper to share my experiences at the infirmary. I wanted to tell Grandmother about bathing patients, making beds with patients still in them, taking temperatures and giving back rubs. I wanted to tell her about the women in long white dresses with black beads hanging down their skirts. The women had radiant, angelic faces framed in white veils that hid their heads and necks. Then there was the man in black who walked up and down the hallways going in and out of rooms as he visited patients and was often followed by one of the women in white, ringing a bell and pushing a cart. Once when they passed me, a nurse gently pushed me to my knees. "The Holy Eucharist is going by," she whispered.

Eucharist? What in the world is a Holy Eucharist? I wondered.

Later as I went from room-to-room, bringing fresh water to the patients, I became acutely aware that a "dead" Man hung on a cross in every room. I knew the cross was a sign of a Christian, but a "dead" Man on the cross? I had never seen this before. Whenever I asked someone about it, the only answer I got was, "It's a Catholic thing." I had never even heard the word "Catholic!" There were no Catholics where I grew up in North Carolina.

Grandmother was the one woman in the world except for my mother that I most loved and admired. I had so many things to tell her about my day at St. Joseph's Infirmary and questions to ask. I knew she would explain the "Catholic" thing! After we had finished our black-eyed peas, rice and corn bread, we cleaned up the kitchen and went out to the front porch. Every evening we sat in the big wicker rockers on the screened porch and talked about all kinds of things until bedtime. There were no streetlights or houses nearby on the little country road, and occasionally a car passed, and a whippoorwill or an owl broke the silence. We watched as fireflies darted through the darkness, and tonight the sounds of beating drums and lively music came from somewhere over the hills from a little church. "Holy Rollers!" Grandmother explained shaking her head.

Finally, I could hold back no longer, "Grandmother, what is a Catholic?"

I waited for an answer. Finally in a rage of anger, Grandmother spoke out, "Don't you ever use that dirty filthy word again or I'll kick you out of my house! You will never be allowed to come back. I'll disown you!" she screamed.

Grandmother got up and went back into the house. She didn't even say, "Goodnight." Stunned I sat a while longer in silence, slowly rocking back and forth. I had never seen Grandmother so angry. I wondered why she was so upset. Finally, I rose from my rocker and went inside the house. Grandmother's bedroom door was closed. Her light was out. I didn't dare disturb her. I got ready and went to bed in the back bedroom where I slept.

The next morning I was up bright and early, dressed in my yellow and white uniform. I walked into the kitchen just as Grandmother came through the back door. She wore a dark blue dress concealed under a red-checkered smock. A red bandana covered her white hair. Grandmother had been out feeding the chickens, the coffee was ready, and two bowls of fresh figs sat at our places on the table. Fresh bread and a toaster sat nearby on a small table. Breaking the silence, I said, "Good morning."

A few seconds later, Grandmother responded in an angry tone. "Remember what I said. Don't you ever say that dirty word again, I meant what I said. You will never be allowed to set foot in my home again! I'll let you keep your job. It is the only one you can find!

But, I warn you don't you dare ask too many questions around St. Joseph's Infirmary!"

I was scared. I was confused. Grandmother had never raised her voice to me. I had always felt like we were buddies, and she knew I would never do anything to hurt or displease her. A few minutes later, we walked out the back door to the carport that was covered with scuppernong grapevines. Grandmother had taken off the smock and removed the bandana. She was every bit a savvy business woman. We got into her green 1950 Ford, which Grandmother was proud that she not only owned, but drove in a day when most women didn't know how to drive. We drove down the country road, past the farms and pastures of cows and horses. Then we passed the East Lake Country Club where someone called Bobby Jones played golf. We passed Grant Park and the Cyclorama where my Great-grandfather, J.C. Flemister, had written and given the original lectures on the famous painting of the Battle of Atlanta during the War Between the States. As we got closer to town, we passed the Capitol and then, the brick wall separating the street from the cemetery where Margaret Mitchell was buried.

Whenever we passed the cemetery, Grandmother always said, "Poor Margaret." Margaret Mitchell had written *Gone with the Wind*. She had been one of Grandmother's dearest friends. They played bridge together every week, before she was hit and killed by a taxi on Peachtree Street in downtown, Atlanta.

Grandmother was a widow. When she was sixteen, she married my grandfather, Harvey James, a history professor at the University of North Carolina. On a speaking tour in the Midwest in 1909, my grandparents stopped over at a hotel in London, Kentucky. My grandfather went down to the corner drugstore to get a Coca-Cola. Someone put arsenic in the drink. He walked out of the store, and fell down in a gutter. Passersby thought he was a drunk. Grandmother went looking for him and when she found him he was dead and had been robbed! Grandmother, who was pregnant with my mother, gave birth prematurely in London, Kentucky.

As soon as Grandmother and the baby could travel, she went back to Georgia. My Grandmother found a room at Widower's Home, a boarding house in Augusta, where she and my infant mother could live. Grandmother worked and put herself through Southern Business School. Ladies at the home took care of my mother.

When not many women worked outside the home, Grandmother founded the "Office Service." She had an idea to rent a large space in the biggest and tallest building in Atlanta, the Healy Building. It was sixteen stories high. She had fifty desks representing companies throughout the States lined up in two rows behind her desk. She answered phones, typed letters and did other secretarial duties for the companies. Outside the government, Grandmother was once the largest user of telephones in the State of Georgia. One whole wall next to her desk was covered with phones. I often saw her with a phone on each shoulder and one in each hand. She was a brilliant business woman.

Grandmother also ran a chicken farm during World War II. I think she supplied half of Atlanta with eggs and chicken when meat was scarce for everyone. She tended the chickens early in the mornings before driving into downtown Atlanta to her office and again after coming home in the evening. No wonder Grandmother was once named "Woman of the Year" in Atlanta.

Grandmother pulled up to the curb and stopped in front of St. Joseph's Infirmary. I got out of the car. "Thank you," I said, as she drove off without a word. A series of thoughts went through my mind. *Was she angry because she could tell how curious I was? Did she understand I had to know what a Catholic was? Would she change her mind about my working at the Infirmary? Why did the word, "Catholic" disturb her so much? And, why did the word, "Catholic" cause my heart to jump with excitement and joy!*

It was planned that since I worked until three o'clock every afternoon that I would walk the eight blocks to the Healy Building and ride home with Grandmother. She closed the office at 5:00

p.m., and I would have extra time to spend researching. Fantastic! I needed to find the answers.

As soon as I clocked in, Sister Bonaventure was waiting for me. "You need to help Emily. She is in room 210. I walked down the hallway to the last door on the left. I gently knocked and slowly opened the door. Horrors of horrors! A man had died! He was on the bed, turned on his side. I had never seen a naked man or a dead one! How embarrassing! Emily was thirty years old. She had had much more experience working as an aide. She explained that we needed to prepare the body for an autopsy before it was taken to the morgue. I dipped cotton balls in the formaldehyde and looking the other way, handed them to Emily who stuffed them in his body.

When we had finished, Emily covered the corpse with a sheet. I suddenly asked in a rush, "Emily, I have to ask you something. What is a Catholic?"

"You're not Catholic? I knew it! I'll explain later. Meet me after work in front of the Sacred Heart Church. It is next door to the Infirmary," she said.

The day could not go by fast enough. At 3:00 p.m. I clocked out, and practically ran next door to the church. Emily was waiting for me. "We are going inside the church," she said. "The best way for me to explain to you about a Catholic, is to show you the church and tell you some of the things Catholics do and why."

"First, we must cover our heads," she instructed. She took a white lace scarf from her purse and put it over her head. Then she took a white linen handkerchief with blue flowers embroidered on it from her pocket. You may use this. I covered my head with the handkerchief. "Ladies cover their heads out of reverence for God," she said. Emily then tugged at the heavy door. It opened to a white marble foyer. "Dip your fingers into this font of water and do as I do," she said. "This is Holy Water. A priest has blessed the water, and we will receive blessings from the water."

I didn't see any blessings in the water! I didn't see anything in the water.

"Cross yourself like this," she continued and demonstrated. "Father, Son and Holy Spirit."

I did as I was told. I knew about the Father, but wondered, *What in the world is a Holy Spirit?*

Grandmother would be furious, yet I could not turn away! My heart pounded, and excitement and joy threatened to overwhelm me! Something was drawing me into the church. What was it? It was impossible to turn back.

Suddenly, we stood in the midst of rows and rows of blazing candles in red glass holders. At first I thought the church was on fire! "We light candles for prayer intentions," Emily explained. She picked up a straw, stuck it into a flame of a candle, once it caught fire she lit a candle. Then she lit another candle with it. "This is for you," she said.

I wondered, *Why?*

I held my breath, as we walked very slowly down the aisle. Emily walked behind me. We passed rows and rows of pews. I looked from side to side. Sunbeams sent myriads of colors and gold particles dancing through stained glass windows. I not only felt the presence of angels, but another Presence was filling me with an indescribable joy! A statue of a beautiful lady adorned in blue standing on a pedestal on a side altar, awakened something deep in my heart. Again I felt a surge of joy, as I wondered, *Who is she?*

Emily called my attention to the sweet aroma of incense. I had never known a place with such beauty, the atmosphere was electric! Silence overwhelmed me with an unfamiliar peace and I felt as if I was in another world. At the end of the aisle, we came to a rail. Emily pointed to a gold box sitting on a table on the other side and whispered, "That is the tabernacle. The Body of Christ, the Holy Eucharist, is inside."

I wondered, *How could this be?*

"We genuflect to Christ whenever we pass in front of it," she said. Emily bowed with her knee touching the floor. Before I could do the same, I looked up.

And that's when it all happened. I suddenly found myself on my knees and I was sobbing uncontrollably. I began calling out urgently I had to know, "Who is He? Who is He?"

The "dead" Man on the cross hung high above the altar. This time He was life-size, and more than that, the "dead" Man had come alive! I felt as if His eyes met mine. In one brief moment the love we shared was enough to know I belonged to Him and Him to me. I had fallen in love with Him, and I did not even know who He was. Desperately, I called out again and again, "Who is He? Who is He?"

I glanced at Emily and I could tell she was terrified of my behavior, not at all expecting this response from me. She took a deep breath and in a calm voice, she answered. "His Name is Jesus."

That night Grandmother and I rocked back and forth on the porch. I wanted desperately to share the events of the day, especially, about what had happened in the Sacred Heart Church, but I knew better. How could I tell her my heart was on fire with love for a man called "Jesus?" Instead I shared that Sister Camille had taught me how to give enemas and how to test the pH in urine.

In my heart I knew I was Catholic even if I wasn't entirely sure what a Catholic was, I only knew I belonged to the "dead" Man on the cross, and I had fallen totally, and irrevocably, in love with Him!

I knew all too well the consequences if my grandmother learned the truth. So, instead the remainder of the summer I told Grandmother I was working a little longer at the Infirmary, when instead I took private catechism lessons from a priest in the rectory. Joy and peace filled my being, as I learned more about the man called "Jesus" and His Church.

BACK TO CONOVER

Summer was over and Grandmother drove me to the bus station. As we hugged one more time before I boarded the bus, I knew in my heart that she loved me, and I of course loved her. I silently prayed for her not to be lonely, as she would be by herself again.

"Promise to write," she said with tears in her eyes.

"Yes, Ma'am," I had answered, fighting back my own tears. Carrying my suitcase, I boarded the Greyhound Bus to Hickory, North Carolina. I left without sharing the truth, I so desperately wanted her to know. I found the source of all joy; but I did not dare.

Daddy would be driving ten miles over from Conover to pick me up at the bus station. The trip would be 185 miles in all, but with the frequent stops to various destinations in-between, the trip would take about seven hours. I would be arriving around 6:00 p.m., and Grandmother had packed a cheese sandwich, some figs and a thermos of hot tea for me to take.

Time on the bus would be well spent as I needed to ponder all that had happened during the summer and my plans for the near future. I was about to enter my senior year at Newton-Conover High, and move to New York City after graduation. How would it all work out? How would I fill the void, in my heart, since I couldn't become a Catholic, yet?

The experience of taking temperatures, assisting doctors and nurses, feeding patients, giving backrubs, and the joy of carrying newborns securely "like footballs," as Sister Bonaventure said, to and from the nursery, had taught me an important lesson. It brought me face-to-face with the sick, their pain and the grief of the dying, but I also witnessed a profound gladness for those who had been healed. I could explain all this to my parents and classmates.

However the deepest lesson I wouldn't be able to share, was the profound faith of so many Catholic patients and their families, who prayed the rosary. If I mentioned the rosary, my family would have no idea what I was talking about as they knew nothing about this form of prayer. There was no way I could explain the "Man on the cross." He had become my constant companion. I felt His Presence wherever I went, and I had fallen in love with Him. My heart and soul belonged to Him. There was no turning back; I had experienced too much joy! There would be no one in Conover with whom I could talk. The word, "Catholic" was not a familiar word with my friends or family. I promised Jesus that every night for the rest of my life, before falling asleep; I mentally would gaze upon Him on the cross.

I had taken secret catechism lessons from the priest. In the beginning it bothered me that I had lied to my grandmother saying I was working a little longer at the infirmary, but the more I learned, the more I felt justified and compelled to someday tell everyone about the Catholic Church. I was overwhelmed with gratitude for the gift of faith that God had given me.

A patient had given me a small rosary. I kept it under my uniform with the crucifix hidden close to my heart all summer, risking that if Grandmother found out, I would be sent back to North Carolina. Another patient had given me two prayer cards, one of the Blessed Mother and the other of the Sacred Heart of Jesus. I kept those hidden, too. Those would be my only sacramentals of the Church for the next nine months.

Sister Mary Aloysius, a patient from Mobile, Alabama was a schoolteacher. She had come to the infirmary for knee surgery. One day when I was making her bed and sprucing up her room, she sensed my anxiety. She asked me if there was anything I would like to talk about. I poured out my heart telling her how desperately I wanted to join the Church, but the priest said I needed more instructions, and I needed to attend a Mass. I wanted to attend a Mass, but there would be no way until I got to New York. I wanted to receive the Holy Eucharist, the true Body and Blood of Jesus. However, I needed to be eighteen to join the church on my own. I was now only sixteen! There was no one else to whom I could have shared my thoughts and feelings. Sister Aloysius listened with so much understanding and love that we arranged to be "pen pals" during the school year, and even after, when I arrived in New York City. She planned to send me the name of a dear priest that would help me. Having her for a pen pal would not be a problem because several other patients wanted to keep in touch, as well. Sister Mary Aloysius was a godsend!

Back home in Conover it was good to be with my mother, father, brothers and sisters. I had not realized how much I had missed them. It was good to be with classmates, and to anticipate all the special activities that were being planned for our senior year.

However, I experienced a profound loneliness. I knew that being alone and talking with Jesus was the only way to fill the spiritual void, in my life. I spent hours weeding the garden, pruning bushes, climbing the old apple tree or sitting high in the cherry tree to be alone with Him. I always felt his Presence. Sometimes I bridled up Bonnie, our horse, who had been discharged from the Army. She had been valuable during World War II and was still quite fit. Her black coat shone in the sunshine, as I grabbed her by her mane and jumped up on her bareback.

As soon as we came to the dirt road near the house, Bonnie knew she was free to gallop at top speed down the old country road. Red dust flew behind us. I held tight to her mane. Eventually, we came to a brook. There I dismantled and led Bonnie into the cool darkness of the nearby woods. Bonnie was content to graze from the patches of grass and drink from the bubbling brook, while I sat on soft green moss and dangled my feet in the cool water.

Looking up at the tall trees, sometimes my eyes filled with tears knowing Jesus had been nailed to one. Then a bird would sing for God's glory, and the bubbling brook seemed to say, as the water danced ever so lightly over stones and crevices, "You have found Jesus!" Once again my joy returned. Then, I climbed up on Bonnie's back, she trotted slowly down the country road to the house. I would miss seeing cows and horses grazing in fields. I would miss seeing Farmer John on his big red tractor. However, I was excited about all the new things I would see!

Many nights after everyone was asleep, I climbed out my bedroom window and sat on the roof that covered the porch below. I sat quietly, thinking and talking with Jesus. Millions of stars filled the black sky. I wondered if the shepherds had seen the same stars when angels sang, "Peace on Earth!" and proclaimed to the world that my Savior had been born. I asked myself over and over, *Why was I chosen to be Catholic? Why isn't everyone Catholic?*

There were only two churches in town, a Missouri Lutheran and a Dutch Reformed. My family tried the Dutch Reformed Church and while I was in eighth grade, I got involved with the Sunday School class and the youth group. I even played the hymns on the piano for them to sing. The cross was taught as a Christian symbol, but no one ever mentioned a man had been on the cross. When I was thirteen, I was brought in front of the congregation, where the pastor baptized me, this was my third time in a different faith! He announced I was a new member and people clapped. Six months later after I memorized the Ten Commandments, I was confirmed. They clapped again!

Mother became unhappy there and we stopped going to the church. Mother often talked about God and called attention to His beauty around us. After I had seen the angel with the children dancing around the tree, when I was three, she had hung a picture of the Guardian Angel with the children in my room. She taught us to say grace at the table, to read a verse from the Bible every night and pray on our knees before getting into bed.

A few days after I was back in Conover, a man came to visit. He was a pastor at a United Lutheran Church several miles out in the country and over the railroad tracks. I sensed Grandmother had been in touch with my mother with a warning to do something about getting Catholicism out of my head. I even overheard Mother telling her it was just a "teenage thing." The pastor invited us to come to his church. I felt helpless. Soon against my wishes, I was baptized for the fourth time and then confirmed for the second time! Grandmother was temporarily satisfied. Mother kept silent never asking me what was in my heart or bringing up anything against or for the Catholic faith. I could not understand why. I consoled myself by knowing I would be free to be Catholic in New York.

My classmates recognized I had changed. They were used to me being involved in many of the school activities. I had been their Homecoming Queen and their Christmas Queen. I had been Captain of the Girls' Basketball Team, President of the Science Club, and played a clarinet in the school band. My priorities had changed. Ball games, dances and even the prom held little excitement for me. Although I dated occasionally, I was dropped when I refused to go steady. I was teased that if a school in the South wasn't good enough for me, then I should go to a "Damn Yankee School". They could not understand why going to New York University was so important. Why couldn't I work my way through a school nearer to home? I could not explain my main motivation was the opportunity to become Catholic.

May 25, 1953 could not come soon enough. That night I marched across the stage with my classmates and received my diploma. A big farewell party was held in the gymnasium. Little did I realize that this was the last time I would see most of my ninety-eight classmates. Some were getting married right away, while others were joining the military. A few were going to college, and some already had jobs in one of the two textile mills in Conover. I however was going to New York City!

Two days later my family and I tearfully hugged each other, as I boarded the train to New York. They did not know that I was actually scared half to death as I had never been to New York or anywhere on my own. Aunt Winnie, Grandmother's sister, whom I had met once, lived in Brooklyn. She would be meeting me at Penn Station. Much to my dismay, I found out Grandmother had asked her to spy on me. If Auntie found out I was mixed up in the Catholic Cult, I would be made to go home. I was seventeen, still too young to legally be on my own or join the Catholic Church.

I had boarded the train at 8:00 p.m. The train would arrive at Penn Station at 4:00 p.m. the next day. Lights were soon turned down and most of the passengers closed their eyes to catch some sleep. I could not sleep. I was too excited. There was too much to think about and I gazed out the window only to see an occasional light in a farmhouse or patches of dark woods, the dark sky however was lit up with stars.

All of a sudden, my arms began to itch! At first I thought it might be the upholstery on the seat. When I could not stop scratching, I got up, and went to the rear of the car where I stood under a light. Poison ivy! It couldn't be. The day before I had taken one last walk through the woods, and I must have come in contact with poison ivy and I went back to my seat thinking I would get calamine lotion as soon as possible. I dozed off, my last thought was, *What a way to start the journey of independence.*

NEW YORK! NEW YORK!

I was glued to the window as the sun came up, my brain slowly registering the foreign landscape. The train roared non-stop through Washington, Baltimore, and Philadelphia. So many trains whizzed by, back and forth on both sides. From New Jersey I made out the skyline of the big city. My heart pounded; never before had I witnessed such tall buildings! Everything went dark, as the train plummeted through the tunnel under the Hudson River. Finally we rolled to a stop at Penn Station right in the heart of Manhattan. I reached for my suitcase from the overhead compartment, and timidly walked down the steps to the train platform. Penn Station was huge and I believed that all of downtown Conover could have easily fit within it! Thousands of people darted back and forth like ants with a purpose, in all directions. This was another world, one I could never have imagined.

I realized I needed to find the Traveler's Aid Booth where Aunt Winnie planned to meet me. After asking several people for directions, I finally found it, yet Auntie had not arrived. Quickly I made my way back across the station and ran up the steps to the outside. I had to find out if it were true that it was hard to see the sky in New York City. I stood on the sidewalk and leaned my head back as far as I could. It was true and I would miss sunrises and sunsets! What about the moon and the stars? What about all the noise from sirens and traffic racing by? I wondered where would I find the solitude my heart craved or the sounds of nature—would I ever hear a bird sing?

I found my way back to the Traveler's Aid Booth, and Auntie still was not there. I stood quietly with my head down. Soon I heard a cackle of laughter, as I looked up I was never so glad to identify that sound, with the welcoming and familiar sight of my Aunt. She had been watching me for several moments and was amused because I looked so scared. She was nothing like her sister, whereas Grandmother was always so serious, Auntie was just the opposite, so full of fun and laughter.

Auntie had a surprise for me, dinner at a restaurant on Times Square—so I could feel the excitement of the city. I carried my suitcase. As I walked a few blocks, with Auntie, she pointed out various sites. My friends back home would not believe I actually stood staring straight up at the Empire State Building, the tallest building in the world! After dinner Times Square transformed into an electrical wonderland! Thousands and thousands of lights of all colors blinked from one area to another. Forty-Second Street was made up of one theater after another. Huge billboards and even a huge waterfall were on top of one of the buildings. Taxicabs raced back and forth, and the people—people darted everywhere. I was enthralled as I took in New York City, which overflowed with energy!

After we ate dinner in an Italian Restaurant on Times Square, we walked down the steps to a nearby subway station. I clung to Auntie's arm, it was scary as I witnessed the train come roaring into the station and screech to a stop. When the doors flew open, we quickly jumped onto the train, heading to Brooklyn where she lived. Auntie laughed when I actually looked out the window, hoping to see fish swim by, while we traveled under the East River. I soon learned she was a tease!

We got off the subway at Sterling Place and walked a few blocks to her apartment, which was small, but delightful and cozy. We would spend fun times there. Auntie was a widow like Grandmother and her husband had died of tuberculosis. She lived alone. Auntie was a designer for the Prestige Handbag Company that created exclusive handbags for special customers, like the Duchess of Windsor.

Auntie only had one small bed, so we pulled out the Castro Sleeper Couch for me. I was so exhausted I could have slept most anywhere. And as soon as my head hit the pillow, I was asleep—when I awoke, it was noon! Auntie had left for work and her note on the kitchen table suggested I eat something from the refrigerator, and she would return around 6:00 p.m. She said that I was not to leave the apartment but she had nothing to worry about—there was no way I planned to leave by myself, until I got my bearings! I was afraid I would get lost.

We spent the weekend together and on Sunday there was no mention of church. I was longing to attend a Catholic Church but it would have to wait. Instead we took a subway to the cemetery on Long Island and placed flowers on her deceased husband, Vern's grave. After dinner we watched *Perry Como* and *The Ed Sullivan Show*, this was my first experience with either of these and it was so exciting. At home we had just gotten our first television set and the shows were from about 4:30-9:30 p.m. and there was only one station. In New York it was the beginning of the golden age of television—and there was much more variety.

We went to bed because early Monday morning I was scheduled to check in at the dormitory and sign up for classes at New York University. It would be a big day for me. That morning Auntie wrote down specific directions for me to follow. First, I would catch the subway, and read the signs to get off at Washington Square, and then go up the steps to the city, from there read street signs which would lead me to the school. She said I was now on my own, and those words both thrilled and excited me! Auntie had to catch a different subway to work.

Once on the subway I carefully watched for my stop and finally, as the train slowed, I read, *Washington Square Park-New York University-Greenwich Village*. This was it! I hurried off and up the steps to the city. The first thing I noticed was a huge arch that I would later learn was the Washington Square Arch, on the north side of a park. Fifth Avenue, the most famous street in Manhattan began at the arch. Behind the arch was the Washington Square Park, which was bordered on the south side by Judson Hall, the dormitory where I was to live and on the east side by New York University's School of Arts and Sciences, where I was to study.

I walked across the park towards a yellow brick building with a tall tower. It turned out to be Judson Hall, the dormitory where I would live. Later I would learn that Edgar Allen Poe had written his famous poem, "The Raven" in the tower room. I was assigned a tiny room with two beds, two dressers, two small desks and a small closet. All the girls on the entire fifth floor would share one bathroom with one shower. No cooking was allowed, although, later I learned to turn an iron upside down, brace it with a metal coat hanger on the corner of a drawer and warm a can of soup.

My roommate, Betsy was a third-year student, from Virginia and studying physical therapy. She was also the president of New York University's Lutheran Club. Why couldn't she be Catholic? The first thing Betsy did was to invite me to join the Lutheran Club! I would soon find out this was in God's plan.

After checking in at Judson Hall, I made my way across Washington Square Park to the Arts and Science Building. The lines to sign up for classes were long, but I did not mind. It was interesting to listen to fellow students speaking in different languages and accents. I would soon learn that my Southern Accent was foreign to them, as well! I had enough money to pay for my first semester classes and the rent for the room at Judson Hall. I had very little money left over for food, so I realized I would have to find a job very soon.

Back at Judson Hall one of the girls in the lounge told me that the University Restaurant on Eighth Street was looking for a hostess. The restaurant was not part of the university, yet was respectable and I vowed to go there the next day. That night a bunch of us walked to a nearby Italian Restaurant. Everything on the menu was foreign to me, and one of the girls suggested pizza. It was my very first pizza! I would soon be introduced to many foods foreign to the South, at that time. I would find out Northerners knew nothing of southern fried chicken or grits!

The next morning was hectic, as I found my way around the University and my classrooms. Later that afternoon I went to the University Restaurant, where I was interviewed by Mr. Gregory, the owner. He asked me to sit down in a booth next to the front desk, where he was counting money. He was thoroughly amused by my Southern Accent, and I was hired on the spot, saying I could start the next day, my hours would be from 5:00-10:00 p.m. six days a week and I would make twenty-one dollars a week and dinner. I learned so much from Mr. Gregory and his wife, who were Greek, they even "adopted" me, often treating me to dinner at the Stork Club, El Morroco, and other famous restaurants, in order to observe how to be a better hostess. Walter Winchell, Teresa Brewer and other famous people frequented these places, yet to me, everyone was special.

One of the orders I received from the owner was to put anyone inappropriately dressed, without a jacket, in the back room sitting at a table with a hot radiator underneath—so they would be uncomfortable and never come back dressed in this way. So, when a gentleman wearing a short sleeved shirt and a lady, fashionably dressed came in, I seated them at that table.

Mere seconds later, my boss came screaming at me, "Do you know who you sat back there?"

"No? Who is it?" *I had no idea who they were.*

"Marlon Brando and Anne St. Marie! Marlon just won an Academy Award for the movie, *On The Waterfront!*"

I stood there dumbfounded and watched as my boss quickly moved the "important" guests to a better table.

After my interview, I left the restaurant. I looked at my watch and realized I had time to find St. Francis of Assisi Roman Catholic Church. I had spoken with Father Arthur Butler on the phone. He told me to come any time before 5:00 p.m., and had given me directions. I caught a bus on Fifth Avenue, got off on Thirty-Second Street and walked west to Seventh Avenue Finally, I found a Catholic Church and my anxious heart pounded! *Catholic—Catholic—Catholic,* I recited over and over again. *At last I can be a real Catholic!*

When I met Sister Mary Aloysius's friend, Father Arthur Butler O.F.M., he agreed to teach me the necessary lessons to join the Catholic Church. I then explained that my great aunt would be spying on me, and if she found out I was mixed up in the "Catholic Cult," as she called it; she would let my grandmother know. Somehow my grandmother had the power to influence my mother, to force me to leave New York. I poured out my heart to this kind man. I had been forbidden to say the word "Catholic," and the only time I had gone inside a Catholic Church, the "Man on the cross" had stolen my heart. I was in love with Jesus! I explained the difficulties I endured my senior year of high school wanting so much to be Catholic and not being allowed to say anything about it. Although I had had some catechism lessons from the priest at St. Joseph's Infirmary, I needed to learn more. My purpose for coming to New York was not only for an education, but to become a Catholic! I was now seventeen, but I knew I needed to be eighteen to legally join the Church on my own. Father Butler said I should go to the Lutheran Club with my roommate, but not get involved. We knew Auntie would be quizzing Betsy and giving my grandmother information.

Then we went next door to the church, I was so excited, I had waited over a year for this moment! The last and only time I had been in a Catholic Church was at Sacred Heart Catholic Church in Atlanta. I had made one last visit to the "Man on the cross" at the end of summer, when I left Atlanta to go back to Conover.

Saint Francis of Assisi Catholic Church did not disappoint me. Again God's presence overwhelmed me and once again tears coursed down my cheeks and my heart nearly burst with joy, as my eyes went to a crucifix hanging in the sanctuary. Jesus my love and constant companion was calling, and leading me, to a deeper relationship with Him, which I would find when I entered the Catholic Church. I was willing to totally surrender. I waited, but not patiently for the day when I would finally become Catholic.

PRECIOUS TIME, PRECIOUS CHILDREN

D elivery trucks, honking taxicabs, and cars clogged the street, while pedestrians dodge traffic, as they jaywalked back and forth. Alarms sound as sidewalk elevators pop-up from the basements below the buildings for the many deliveries being made to the restaurants, bars and nightclubs. Aromas of onions, garlic and other enticing foods being prepared for diners, season the air. It is nine o'clock in the morning, in New York City.

At night, Eighth Street becomes transformed, taking on a whole new look. It is located in the heart of Greenwich Village in lower Manhattan, where you find New York University's Washington Square School of Arts, and Sciences. Flashing neon lights entice ladies and gentlemen, dressed in their finery for a glamorous evening of dining and entertainment. Ladies arrive in slinky gowns and furs, gentlemen in tuxedos. Some patrons kept their heads down, as they pass racy photos and descend the concrete stairs to visit strip clubs.

The University Restaurant, where I worked as a hostess, seemed out of place on this street. It was opened for lunch and dinner. By ten p.m. when Eighth Street was coming alive with the night crowd, the patrons and personnel of the popular, conservative restaurant frequented by business executives, professors and even the Chancellor of New York University had departed, the restaurant was closed for the night.

One day as I walked towards the restaurant, I suddenly heard a loud and angry voice that shouted, "Get out of here, you nasty kids! Don't come back! I'll call the cops!" Without warning, four filthy, barefoot children, all about five or six years old, raced up concrete steps from a basement bar. I grabbed a railing, steadying myself, trying not to fall, as they each bumped into me.

"Look what we have! Two nickels! We are rich!" the children cried in unison, as one of the boys proudly held out a dirty palm displaying the coins for me to see.

Gathering my composure, I inquired, "Where did you get the nickels?"

"From men in the bar," one answered.

"Men in bars always give us money," a little girl answered.

I could see they were not afraid of strangers. "Where are your mothers and fathers?" I asked.

They all giggled, as they answered in unison, "Working! Sleeping! We don't know!" One grinned showing a missing tooth.

Tears filled my eyes. I wanted to gather them in my arms. My heart ached as I witnessed these children in need, dirty and barefoot, running in and out of bars, begging for money. *How appalling!* I thought. *Dear, Jesus, I prayed, I know we are all children of God. How can I help them?*

I always knew where my parents were, and my parents always knew where I was and what I was doing. Things had been scarce back in Conover, North Carolina where I grew up during World War II, but I had never seen children begging. My town didn't even have a bar! *Jesus, what can I do?* I pleaded again.

The next few days, as I walked around Greenwich Village, I saw many children roaming the streets, playing in gutters, chasing up and down fire escapes, picking garbage cans, and dodging cars in the streets. Most of these children were not homeless. Some parents worked all-night and slept all day. Many were immigrants trying to eke out the American dream. Children were left to fend for themselves.

As I walked past a church, I suddenly turned around and went back. A sign in front of the church read, "Saint John's Evangelical Lutheran Church, Re-opening Soon. All Are Welcome." An idea popped into my head. *God, is this from you? This is a Lutheran Church. I'm becoming a Catholic!*

I assumed the red brick residency next door to the church was a rectory; I walked up the steps and rang the bell. A young lady answered. She introduced herself as the pastor's wife and invited me to come into the parlor. A few seconds later a young man trailed by two toddlers came down the hallway.

He introduced himself as Pastor Jim and invited me into his office. He said that the church had been closed during the World War II, and many of their parishioners had moved away. He wanted to revive the church. At one time the church had boasted the largest Sunday school in all of Manhattan.

I explained to Pastor Jim that I wanted to start a children's club for the street children. I shared my experience of working with my mother during the War. I had been trained in arts and crafts, childcare and even to evacuate the whole town if necessary. I gave him my schedule; I had time from two to four o'clock on Saturday afternoons.

"Well, I'm just starting to re-open the church. I don't even know my way around the city yet, but I accept your offer of help. Maybe you can invite the children to come to Sunday school," he suggested.

Sure!" I answered enthusiastically, adding, "They need to learn about the Man on the cross. Pastor Jim looked surprised. If only he knew that the Man on the cross at the Sacred Heart Church in Atlanta had stolen my heart.

We walked next door to the church hall. It was perfect with plenty of space, tables, chairs, and a small kitchen. The children's club would start in two weeks. I was ecstatic!

Again, I walked around Greenwich Village. This time I invited every street child I saw to join the club. I gave them all a slip of paper with the information. I even recruited four "street" teenagers to help me.

On opening day Pastor Jim was as excited as I was, to see over forty children from different nationalities, come to the church hall. Soon over sixty children would be regulars. They listened to Bible Stories, made arts and crafts, sang songs, played games, and enjoyed simple refreshments that I provided on my meager earnings.

One Sunday morning when the first Sunday school class began, I was the only teacher. I was so happy to tell them about a man called Jesus who loved them and was always with them.

I told the children to bring their Bibles for the following Sunday. They all gave me blank stares. I found out that not one of them had a Bible. All of the friends I grew up with back home had Bibles, we considered the Bible the most important book of all. I phoned my Mother, and she was astounded to learn that the children did not own Bibles. In a few weeks, the ladies of her church guild sent us over a hundred, mostly used, Bibles. Some even had notes to the children in them. The children were delighted. And, Pastor Jim was ecstatic!

One day I took fourteen of the children on a field trip to the Bronx Zoo. Some had never been more than a few blocks from where they lived. Some had not been on a subway, let alone a forty-five minute ride up Manhattan. We got off at the Bronx Zoo Station and walked up the steps toward the front.

A ten-year-old girl from Sweden, with blond braids wrapped around her head suddenly yelled excitedly pointing, "Is that a tree?"

Dumbfounded I answered, "Yes."

She had never been to a park, even though there was one only a few blocks from where she lived. We stood under a very large maple tree with huge limbs and green leaves glistening in the morning sun. The children looked up and watched birds fluttering and chirping, as they flew from limb to limb. Back home I would have climbed the tree, but these children would not have that experience!

The rest of the morning held more surprises for me. Chickens and cows were farm animals to me, but now they were fenced in just like the jungle animals. Some of the children could not believe chickens gave us eggs, and cows gave us milk! In the animal petting area, they squealed as they petted rabbits, sheep and goats. Lions, tigers, zebras and all the other jungle animals fascinated them as well, but the highlight of the trip was when they were given an elephant ride! Their eyes lighted up with excitement when we took a tour of the Botanical Gardens, and the children smelled every flower!

Before we headed back to the subway and Greenwich Village, we had a picnic of peanut butter and jelly sandwiches that I had brought along. The children got soaking wet running and screaming with laughter, as they ran through a nearby fountain. They took turns as I pushed them on the swings to dry out.

We then headed back to the subway station and Greenwich Village, the children said they would never forget that day, and neither would I. All these years later I still recall the events with clarity.

Another day I was busy checking tissue cultures in the lab where I worked at the University. I received a phone call from an irritated librarian in the building across the street. "Are you Miss Biggers? Do you know anything about a children's club?" she shouted over the phone

Stunned, I answered, "Yes, of course I do."

"Well, there are children running through the library and the hallways disturbing the classrooms. They say they are looking for you. Come get them!" she demanded.

As fast as I could, I threw off my lab coat, surgical mask and cap and I ran down the stairs, across the street and up the stairs to the second floor of the other building. An angry security guard had the children in custody.

"Children, come with me, at once!" They could see I was upset as I led them back down the stairs and across the street to a bench in Washington Square Park. I could lose my job, but more importantly, these children had ventured so far from their neighborhoods and it was a dangerous trek.

"Don't you ever come here again!" I scolded. "You will get us all in trouble!"

"But, we wanted to see you," they all answered in unison.

"I'll see you on Saturday. Now go home!" I ordered. I watched them slowly walk away, their heads hung low. I didn't like to be firm with them, but it was for their safety as well as my job security.

Later, I walked through the front door of the Sage House, a forerunner of the YWCA, the women's boarding house, where I lived. The housemother called me into her office. She said that afternoon a group of raggedy kids had left a box of things for me.

"They said to tell you that they were sorry."

I looked into the box, and my eyes welled up with tears. There was a doll with one arm, a broken jack-in-the-box, a worn out top, a well-used jump rope, a ripped comic book and several other items. Tears coursed down my cheeks, as I explained to the housemother what had happened that afternoon at the University. The children had brought me their most prized possessions in hopes of forgiveness. If they only knew how dearly I loved them!

These were precious days with precious children. Once when the children and I were serving coffee and doughnuts to the elderly congregation, one of the little girls kept snitching doughnuts. I finally asked her what she had eaten for breakfast. She responded that she had not eaten in three days. I took her home with me to the Sage House. I asked the housemother to give the little girl my dinner. The housemother was kind enough to give us both dinners.

Whenever I could, I visited the children where they lived, especially if I knew one was ill. One little black girl and her mother called me their angel. I called them angels as well. Once when visiting a child who was sleeping on a mattress on the floor, the mother insisted on making me coffee. She said that she always used the same coffee grounds at least six times, and the coffee she was making me was the fifth time. I was grateful that she shared her meager offerings. However, I got more than coffee that day.

One Sunday afternoon at a Christmas Concert in the church, I was listening to Handel's Messiah and sitting in a pew, halfway down the aisle. Suddenly, an usher leaned over to me and whispered. I looked to the side and there stood two little girls, barefoot, dirty, and wearing almost nothing. It was freezing outside! Snow was a foot deep and still falling down. I could only think of the story of the "Little Match Girl" who froze to death and was carried away by angels. *Surely, these little girls would go straight to Heaven*, I thought.

I took off my coat, walked over to the shivering little girls and wrapped my coat around them, as I lead them to the back of the church. A little bit later, the concert took a break. Somehow, we were noticed by the entire congregation! A Good Samaritan gave me money to take them home in a cab. Later the ladies of the church put together food baskets and gifts, which were taken to the addresses I gave them. How good God is to touch our hearts to love and help one another, especially children our most precious gifts.

I ran the children's club for five and a half years, even after I joined the Catholic Church. The pastor was pleased his congregation was growing and children continued to come to Sunday school, and now there were more teachers. I think the pastor secretly hoped to convert me from Catholicism, because he gave me the book, "Here I Stand" about Martin Luther.

I shared with Pastor Jim my great love for the Man on the cross and the greatest gift to mankind, the Holy Eucharist. He saw my joy, although he did not understand it. We would remain friends and I often prayed for him.

Father Butler was informed every week of my involvement with the children's club at the Lutheran Church, while I was waiting to be old enough to join the Catholic Church. I was glad my aunt told my grandmother I was involved in the Lutheran Church. However, I was spending every free moment at Saint Francis of Assisi, St.

Patrick's Cathedral or the Cloisters, which was a museum of Catholic artifacts. And, each day I fell more in love with, Jesus the Man on the cross and His Catholic Church.

NEW BEGINNINGS

The first week of May had arrived and the semester was coming to an end with only one more exam looming. However, this was the least of my concerns, as I finally decided to write my grandmother and explain why I would soon be joining the Catholic Church. I was now eighteen-years-old and could join on my own without parental consent. I wrote her that there was no turning back, I was called to be Catholic, and my heart and soul were literally alive with the joy of the Holy Spirit!

Grandmother wrote back, and she was beside herself with anger. First she blamed Auntie for not keeping a closer watch over me, and then she accused Catholics—in general, of many atrocities, which I would never repeat. She blamed me for being ungrateful and disrespectful to her judgment, and she blamed Mother for letting me go to New York and left to my own devices. To appease Grandmother, my mother sent me literature on the Methodist Church; otherwise, Mother said nothing else, and I always wondered, *why*? It would be many years later that I would learn the reason she didn't protest.

The New York University Lutheran Club was hosting one last meeting, actually a gathering of about eighteen clubs from colleges and universities around the Metropolitan Area of New York

City. The students would be celebrating the end of the year and announcing plans for the next year. I had faithfully attended the New York University Lutheran Club meetings, as Father Butler had suggested, and I had been careful not be involved in any way except for my presence. The danger of my being made to leave New York was a real threat when I was underage, and I learned that Auntie had frequent conversations with my roommate and so had kept tabs on my activities and was confident I had given up the idea of being a Catholic.

The conference hall was overflowing with dozens of students. My roommate would soon be graduating and I felt uneasy, as she looked at me with a twinkle in her eye and ascended the steps to the stage where several pastors were sitting in a row. She gave a welcome to visiting students, and then, she announced that the Board of Officers of the New York University's Lutheran Club had chosen new officers for the coming year. She began announcing the officers. Then, horror of horrors—I heard loud and clear, that I, Betty Biggers, had unanimously been selected to be the incoming president.

I nearly panicked as I stood up from my chair and slowly walked up the steps to the stage to face a sea of cheering students. I took the microphone, and announced clearly, "I cannot be president."

"We will help you!' replied one of the pastors on stage.

"I can't!" I replied firmly.

"But, why?" the pastor insisted.

"Because on June 5th, I am joining the Catholic Church," I said in a loud, clear voice.

There was dead silence, and a pastor took the microphone and asked, "What did we do wrong?"

"I don't know," I said, "But the Catholic Church has done everything right."

The rally was ruined. I was shunned as some of the participants actually turned their backs to me, and no one would speak to me further. I let myself out a side door. Slowly I walked across Washington Square Park and back to the dormitory. I would miss the company of some of my friends. My roommate would not even sleep in the same room that night; however I was flooded with joy. I was now free to be Catholic!

I also had a predicament that I had to vacate my room at the dormitory and find a place to live in less than two weeks. I could not stay in the dormitory unless I was taking classes. And on top of that, I needed to work during the summer and save money for fall classes. Father called the Mother Superior of Our Lady of Peace Convent on West Fourteenth Street in Manhattan. There were no vacancies in the women's residence run by the French Canadian Nuns, but when Father Butler explained to them I was soon joining the Church, they made room for me in the convent!

My room was tiny—the same size the nuns had, which contained a bed, a dresser and a small desk. Two hooks were on the wall to hang up my clothes, and I would be sharing the bathroom with the nuns. I had to be exceptionally silent and have a curfew of 9:00 p.m., because the front door had no keyhole, and there would be no one to let me into the building. Mother Superior was tiny about five feet tall, and spoke only French, which I didn't speak, however I was so grateful again to be among veiled women with radiant faces, long dresses and beads hanging down their sides. We communicated through the Spirit!

Father Butler asked Mother Superior to find me a sponsor for my upcoming baptism. I had no Catholic acquaintances because of my necessary secrecy. Mother Superior introduced two girls to me who lived in the residence that the nuns operated and both were in Broadway shows. Both were devout Catholics and agreed immediately to sponsor me.

June 5, 1954 was a very special day for me. I met the girls in the parlor of the convent, and we walked twelve blocks to Saint Francis of Assisi Catholic Church. My heart pounded with excitement all the way, the girls were excited, too. Father Butler was waiting for us in the lower chapel and he directed me into a confessional. "Your sins are forgiven you," would become my favorite words.

Father Butler and I stood at a large white marble font of water, flanked by my sponsors. This time I knew this was blessed water, not like the day I first encountered a font of Holy Water at the Sacred Heart Church in Atlanta and had no idea what it symbolized.

As Father Butler poured water over my head, I remember his hand trembling, as it became the Hand of God, anointing me in the *Name of the Father, the Son and the Holy Spirit*. I was totally zapped by the Holy Spirit as I was baptized for the fifth and last time! Catholic! It was the greatest day of my life!

When Father Butler placed the Holy Eucharist on my tongue, I looked up—and there was Jesus, the Man on the cross, my Lord and Savior—He was not dead, but alive to me spiritually! He looked into my soul. I almost laughed out loud. I was now totally His and Catholic! From that day forward, whenever I hear the word, "Catholic," I thank God for His grace of *bringing me home*.

Back at the convent, Mother Superior and the other nuns prepared a celebration luncheon. They had invited all the 168 ladies from the residence to join us. I had never received so many hugs in my life! What a day to rejoice with all of my fellow Catholics and new found friends! I lost my Lutheran friends but gained so many more—the Lord provided for me that day, since I didn't have my family or close friends to celebrate with me.

All the waiting, the scolding by my grandmother, the secrecy, the loneliness, and even the final abandonment had been worth arriving at this moment in time. I knew I would never be the same—I would now be all I should be, as a Catholic! Yes, I had been totally zapped, not by lightning this time but by the Holy Spirit!

STARVING AND SURVIVING

M y second floor room in the convent looked out over the always busy and noisy, West Fourteenth Street. Directly across the street and on a second floor balcony, patrons sat at tables covered with red-checkered cloths, toasting one another with glasses of wine. An aroma of Spanish spices came from the restaurant, and seemed to dance into my room and right under my nose with the gaiety of the lively Tarantella. I could not help whirling around and laughing aloud. I was deliriously happy; I was finally Catholic!

I gingerly peeked out the door of my room, and saw a long hallway lined with closed doors. One of the nuns was just getting off the ancient self-pulled elevator that looked like a small cage. Quietly, she disappeared behind one of the doors. Silence inside the convent was deafening. The French Canadian Nuns, who dressed in black dresses and veils with a border of white pleats around their smiling faces, seemed to glide through the hallway, up and down the stairs, and through the corridors going back-and-forth to the other building that was home to 168 women boarders. I felt God's presence and His angels everywhere within these walls.

Breakfast and dinner were served in the dining room of the ladies residence. To get to the dining room, I walked down a glass-paneled corridor that passed by the nuns' private chapel. I loved to hear their angelic voices, raised in praise to God, which was often accompanied by the scent of sweet incense which filled the air. Sometimes I lingered outside the closed doors, and at times one of the nuns would see me and beckon me to come in and join them. I would sit quietly and gaze at Jesus, the Man on the cross, always remembering that first experience at the Sacred Heart Church in Atlanta, when I realized I belonged to him. He was my constant companion, always in my heart and mind. His love had changed my life forever.

A statue of a beautiful lady in blue with a crown of gold stars stood on a pedestal near the sanctuary. I had seen a similar statue of the lady in the Sacred Heart Church in Atlanta. I was told it was a statue of Mary. I had grown up knowing only that Mary rode a donkey and gave birth to Jesus, but nothing else. Now, I reasoned that the Mother of Jesus was no ordinary person. I vowed to learn more about her. I would later learn Mary is the Mother of God, because Jesus is God—a Doctrine of the faith determined at the Council of Nicaea in 317 A.D. She was my mother, too—and I learned about the "saints." I was excited to learn that we are all called to be saints and wanted to learn more.

I thought, *Really? Real saints? How could anyone be a saint? Who decided if one was a saint? Were they not just ordinary people?*

I learned about St. Patrick on the morning I wore an orange blouse to breakfast in the dining room. It was St. Patrick's Day, and everyone else was wearing green! That was the day I learned that St. Patrick was Irish, and he used a shamrock, which has three leaves, to teach about the Trinity. There was so much to learn and experience about the rich Catholic faith, it was full of history and pointed all to learn more about our God!

At this point I realized I had to buckle down and find ways to make money. The fall semester would be here before I knew it and there was no time to relax or waste. I soon found myself again, face-to-face with nuns when I became a circulating aide in the operating rooms of St. Vincent's Hospital located in Greenwich Village. These nuns were like the nuns at St. Joseph's Infirmary in Atlanta; they were nurses and wore white. Their undying devotion, to those in need, their compassion and love for the sick, elderly, and underprivileged taught me so much about how the love of God can work through us, if we let Him. I frequently spent extra time volunteering in the charity ward, where the homeless, less fortunate and non-English speaking poor lay helplessly in their beds. Whatever I did for them, I was often rewarded with a smile and those smiles touched my heart with joy.

One morning one of the nuns in the convent tapped on my door. She had come to sweep my room, and I'm so glad I was home! When she reached under my bed with her broom, she pulled out a rat skin floating in a small basin of formaldehyde. The nun was hysterical! I finally made her understand that I was working on a project for a biology class at the University; she smiled nervously and quickly left my room.

In a biology class at NYU, I had been studying anatomy of various species. Students were not supposed to take any parts of the specimens out of the laboratory, but I had sneaked the skins of a ten inch earthworm and a frog out of class, stuffed them and covered them with clear nail polish. They looked alive again! Even I was impressed with my taxidermy skills. Back home in North Carolina, I had once wired the bones of our Thanksgiving turkey together; and now I had also wired a lobster together. The rat skin compelled me to use my taxidermy skills on him, but it was a challenge because I really hated rats!

After I had stuffed and sewn up the rat skin, I glued small black beads into the eye sockets. Amazingly, the rat looked real. I was so happy with the results that I decided to show my professor, even though I feared the consequences. I packed the reconstructed specimens and took them back to class, where I apologized profusely and asked the professor's forgiveness for taking the remnant pieces of the specimens out of the lab. My professor, who happened to be the Chairman of the Biology Department, was impressed rather than upset. And this turned into a job offer, of an hour or two a day, washing test tubes in the laboratory where he and others were conducting experiments for cancer research. I said yes to every job, no matter how big or small because every penny I could earn was needed.

At the beginning of the summer, the professor gave me a book on tissue culture with the proposal to replace his tissue culturist, who was leaving. If I would study and learn the techniques by the end of the summer, I could have the job of a lady who had a PhD!

Not only would I be immersed in research, growing cells from ovarian tumors obtained from NYU's Belleview Hospital, and cultivating cancerous kidney cells from frogs; I would receive a decent salary and the cost of my classes would be cut in half. What an opportunity!

During the summer I found more ways to make extra money. On Sunday afternoons I became a mail order operator for Macy's Department Store, and a local chemical company offered a small stipend to students to have cosmetic patch tests done on their arms. I signed up! Later I was asked to wash each side of my face three times a day for ten days with two popular brands of soaps, but after three days both sides of my face were swollen and broken out. My arms were a mess with red spots! The chemical company called off the experiments, and I went home with fifty dollars.

I continued to wash test tubes through the summer and was thankful for the job. I diligently studied the book on tissue culture. I had to quit the hostess job at the restaurant because I had difficulty getting back to the convent by 9:00 p.m., when the doors closed. Once I had to spend a night sitting on a park bench until dawn. It was spooky!

Things were rough financially, although I was never unhappy. I trusted that God had a plan. I began patching my shoes with cardboard and lived for six weeks eating only half a can of soup a day that I warmed over a Bunsen burner in the lab when no one was looking. I lost twenty-five pounds!

Every morning, as I walked through Washington Square Park to classes or work, I saw sunlight dancing through the trees and once again, remembered my mother's favorite saying, "Smile and the world smiles with you. Weep and you weep alone." I kept smiling. I didn't want anyone to know about my financial predicament, and my family didn't have money to spare.

My sister Dot came for a visit and noticed I was extremely thin. She suggested I try modeling. I didn't wear makeup and knew nothing about the latest fashions; however I decided to give it a try. Helen Frazier, founder of the Barbizon Modeling School saw potential in me. She said I had high cheekbones, a long neck and being five-seven was an asset.

After a series of classes, I graduated from the Barbizon Modeling School and I received a contract from the Francis Gill Agency! Surprisingly, my family was very happy and supportive. Francis Gill had strict rules consisting of: no smoking, no drinking, no cussing, and no indecent exposure. She told me it was important to always be like the "girl next door" or top clients would not hire me. I would not have difficulty, and truthfully was very happy and relieved to hear her rules.

Soon I was walking runways, wearing the latest fashions, and being photographed by leading photographers. I studied speech at Carnegie Hall and learned how to suppress my southern accent. I found myself in demand as a spokeswoman for television commercials.

I began taking fabulous trips to places like Paris, London, Bermuda, the Dominican Republic, Haiti and Nassau. Everywhere I traveled I searched for the Catholic Churches and found each one, more beautiful than the next. Wherever I went, I found His Presence.

There were many opportunities to go astray. There were invitations to fancy restaurants, shows or exquisite weekends with clients. One girl bragged that a man, who was not a steady, had given her a three thousand dollar diamond pin she wore. Jewelry held little interest for me except for the crucifix I have always worn around my neck. My dates were always with the Man on the cross, He had given me my most cherished gift of all—the Catholic Faith. It was the Catholic Church and its teachings that kept me protected in the midst of all this worldliness. My social life was pretty dull by almost everyone else's standards.

At the end of the summer I learned all I needed to know about tissue culture, to my professor's satisfaction and I was hired and became a member of the Faculty of the Biology Department of New York University's Washington Square School of Arts and Sciences. I was one of the youngest members to be accepted to New York's Academy of Sciences. Besides growing cancer cells, I assisted my professor in the Microbiology Classes and began taking classes in the Master's Degree Program.

When I was not working or taking classes, I was at church, either at St. Francis of Assisi Catholic Church, or St. Patrick's Cathedral. Sometimes I took a ride on a subway to upper Manhattan and spent a Sunday afternoon at the Cloisters, which contained a museum of Catholic artifacts, and I was happy to just sit and listen to Gregorian Chants.

Modeling, growing tissue cultures and taking classes were all compatible because I was free to make my own schedules, which I found myself juggling often. After living in the convent for eight months, I finally found another place to live at the Sage House, a Christian Women's Boarding House. It was located a few blocks from the University. I had lived at the convent longer than I planned, and the nuns and I tearfully hugged as I moved out. Never would I forget them. The Sage House turned out to be noisy and not conducive for studying or sleeping. A few months later my friend Heidi, who also lived at the Sage House and I rented an apartment in a brownstone building, two doors away. Heidi made a decent salary as a secretary, and I had finally started to make ends meet.

Heidi was in her thirties and had arrived from Heidelberg, Germany after World War II. As a young girl, she had spent three months in solitary confinement with no light for "mouthing off" to a Nazi Officer. Once a day the door to her cell was opened, and a cup of water and a piece of bread were shoved into the dark room. While she was there, rats ran over her, and she became very ill with no one to help her. Her four brothers had refused to join the Nazi Army until their mother and father were pushed to their knees with guns pointed at their heads and threatened with execution, if her brothers did not join. Heidi made me understand that there is nothing worse than fighting for a cause you do not believe in. The real crime Heidi and her brothers were guilty of was being Catholic-Christians! Yes, I had cried myself to sleep many nights during World War II, but so had many others, like Heidi far away in Germany. She believed Catholics were pilgrims in God's Army, and we must stand up for our Church and fight for the teachings of Christ. Not only was my education growing but my spiritual life as well.

ALONE AND SCARED

I leaned over the microscope to view the ovarian cancerous tissue that I had been cultivating for the last week. Then I slid one last slide under my microscope. My supervisor, the Biology Department head, was pleased he had hired me. He was esteemed in his own right as a member of the Damon Runyon Cancer Foundation—and had very high expectations for me. I knew he would be very pleased to see the new growth from this latest tumor, which would help with the research and determination as to treatment. I jotted down my findings in my notebook and looked at the clock. It was 10:00 p.m.!

Oh, no! Why did I stay so late? I thought. I usually left the laboratory by 8:00 p.m.

I needed to check the slides, I reasoned with myself, trying to justify the time. I was worried because I knew I was going to be walking alone in the night. As I made one last inspection of the lab, I pulled off my white cap and surgical mask and laid them next to my microscope. Everything was in order. I turned off the lights and walked out into the hallway and around the corner to the elevator. Normally, the hallway was bustling with students and professors rushing back and forth. Tonight the hallway was dark and silent.

It was eerie and I felt uneasy. It seemed like an eternity for the elevator to arrive to the third floor.

"Good evening," I said as Tom the elevator operator opened the door and I entered.

"You're late tonight," he said, "You're the only one left in the entire building, and usually on Saturday nights nobody is here but me," he admonished.

I had no answer. It was true, normally I left hours earlier. The elevator stopped at the ground floor. I stepped out. "Thanks, Tom." I said, as we walked across the dimly lit lobby to the security door. He unlocked the door and let me out closing it securely behind me. I walked down the block and across the street into Washington Square Park in Greenwich Village, which despite the hour was always bustling in the evenings, and into the early mornings with entertainers and onlookers. I was glad to see people. Ballet dancers whirled around the fountain. One man sang "Figaro," as he pedaled a unicycle through the park. A longhaired young man strummed a guitar. Artists displayed their paintings with hopes of selling them, and entertainers held out cups to collect coins from onlookers. Most were hoping to be "discovered."

As I approached the Washington Square Arch, which marks the southern beginning of Fifth Avenue, I glanced up at the marble statue of Giuseppe Garibaldi, an Italian military hero, and I smiled. Even at night pigeons sat on his head and shoulders. Then I noticed a young man in his twenties was leaning against the marble base. *Was he staring at me? Why?*

Walking quickly, I pretended not to see the man. I passed under the arch, onto Fifth Avenue and headed toward Ninth Street two blocks away where I shared a two-bedroom apartment on the third floor of a four-story brownstone building. The neighborhood had seemed safe when my friend, Heidi, and I chose to live there. It was a few doors down from the well-known Fifth Avenue Hotel where many prestigious people lived and stayed.

The walk seemed extra-long that night. I wanted to get safely to my apartment, sensing that I was now being followed, and I didn't dare look back. Then, I remembered my roommate, Heidi was away in Pennsylvania. The landlord who occupied the first floor was with his family on Long Island. The interior designers who lived on the second floor were on a buying trip in Australia. The two NYU law students, Mark and Greg, who rented the top floor, were also away. That meant I would be the only one in the building that night. I swallowed hard and thought to myself, *I'll be fine.*

God, protect me, I prayed. *Send my guardian angel to comfort me.* I immediately felt better.

To enter the building I had to go through two sets of glass doors, the first set was always unlocked. Visitors would ring a buzzer in the small foyer to be let in by a tenant who was in an apartment. The second set of doors was always locked, tenants had keys. I walked up the three steps to the entrance of my building and let myself into the foyer. *Why was I so nervous?* I wondered about the man, and had the sense that he was behind me somewhere close. I fumbled in my purse for the key to the door, found it and quickly unlocked the second set of security doors. As I pulled the doors closed, I looked—and there was the man standing on the sidewalk. It was the same man I had seen in the park! He was looking at me with an expressionless stare. Quickly, I jerked the doors to make sure they were securely locked behind me. I started up the first flight of stairs.

As I approached the landing on the second floor, I heard noises coming from the front door. My heart raced. Surely, if it was that man, he couldn't get in; I started up the second flight. Now, I heard someone running up the stairs below. I reached my landing and turned to see that man approaching the top of the stairs.

My whole body seemed to be going numb with a sense of danger, but I managed to turn and ask, "Are you going up to see the students?"

"Wouldn't you like to know," he said in a low voice.

As I walked towards the door to my apartment, I turned again to look at him. He now stood staring at me. In one hand he held up a black club. In the other hand he held up two leather strings.

Suddenly, he jumped towards me. I held up my arm to stop a blow from the club. I let out a blood-cuddling scream. "God, help me!" I cried out.

A loud shout rang out, "What's going on down there?" Mark, one of the graduate students, flew down the stairs. My attacker shoved me to the floor and took off. Mark, helped me up and into my apartment, I was so happy he wasn't away as I thought! Physically the attacker had not hurt me, but emotionally I was a wreck! I cried and shook uncontrollably.

Mark called the police, and a few minutes later my apartment was swarming with policemen and detectives. I gave them a detailed description of the man and a thorough account of the incident, starting with first seeing the man in the park. Detectives searched my apartment and the building for any evidence that could be helpful. They fingerprinted the railing on the stairs. They picked up the leather strings and black club that had been left by the attacker.

"Young lady, you are very lucky. There have been a lot of incidents around here in the last few weeks. Members of a gang here in Greenwich Village take turns watching for single women, and then one of them attacks," he said.

"We will be back in touch with you," another detective added. "Try not to be out alone at night by yourself."

"And keep your door locked," another policeman admonished. "You could have been history!" The policemen and detectives then left.

"Thank you, Mark! You saved my life." I said, still suffering from shock, trembling and crying. I assured Mark I could stay that night in the apartment by myself. The policemen left me a phone number, and so had Mark.

"Call me if you need anything," Mark said as he walked back upstairs.

That night I couldn't sleep. I kept imagining that the doorknob was turning. I was too scared to look in my closet or pull the shower curtain back. I shook and cried. I also thanked God that

He had heard my plea for help and sent Mark to my rescue. It was a miracle that Mark had been home. He had planned to go skiing in Vermont with his roommate for the weekend, but changed his mind at the last minute to stay home and study.

Mark came down to my apartment early the next morning. He could tell I was frazzled and had not slept. My eyes were red and swollen from crying. He insisted that I spend the day with him and his girlfriend. I was glad to not be alone.

When Heidi came home from Pennsylvania that night, she was horrified after hearing what had happened to me. "I have to move," I told Heidi at the end of the week. "I can't sleep. I hear noises. I imagine I'm being followed. On the street I look down when I walk. If I look up, I'm afraid I'll see his horrible, evil eyes looking at me again."

Heidi understood that I had to move, but she liked the apartment and had a girlfriend that worked with her who had asked to share the apartment, if I ever left. It was agreed that I would find another place, but not in the same neighborhood.

Two weeks later I received a phone call from the police station. A detective had identified and caught a man that met my description, the man admitted to attacking me. He was being held for beating a woman to death with a chain and stabbing her husband. I wasn't needed at the station, but the police would be in touch if things changed. I was glad not to face that man again. *Please let this be the end of it*, I prayed. I knew God had kept me safe, and I knew God would help me find a safe place to live.

Although, I knew the man had been caught, for many years—and, even today, the thought of what might have happened haunts me. I often imagined I saw the man again on a subway platform, standing on a street corner or following me. I praise God that I was spared and that I could pray for those who suffer.

ED SULLIVAN TO MY RESCUE

N ot many women can say they have taken a bath on national television, but I can. It happened on a Sunday in November in the year 1957. Most of that morning had been spent rehearsing for *The Ed Sullivan Show* that was to air that evening at eight o'clock. In the fifties, television shows and commercials were shown live, and believe me the rehearsals were intense. When cameras rolled before a live audience there could be no mistakes.

Unfortunately, mistakes did happen. Once when I was doing a *West Clock* television commercial, I took a golf swing to show off a sports watch. The camera then panned over to a young lady who was to say something about the watch, where they found her sound asleep on a bale of hay!

For my scene on *The Ed Sullivan Show* that night, I would be sitting in a bathtub with a towel wrapped around my head, pretending to take a bath, while dreaming about Tony Bennett. Tony was the guest star on the show that evening, who would sing his hit, "Because of You." In reality, I was fully dressed, wearing a strapless blouse, and there was no water in the tub. The television audience would have to use their imaginations, as Ed Sullivan was a very moral man and a devoted Irish Catholic. Nothing even remotely scandalous would happen on his show.

After that scene on the stage, I was to get out of the tub, and joined by nine other models. Ed Sullivan would then introduce us as the Top Ten Models in the USA, and give a short biography of each of us. All of my friends and family would be able to see me back home in North Carolina.

Ed Sullivan was familiar with me from the other skits I had performed on his past shows. On one show Caesarea Giuseppe, the famous opera star from Italy sang to me as we danced a waltz. I did a skit with James Arness who was best known for the part he played as Matt Dillon, the star on the Gun Smoke Series. James was tall and impressive, wearing boots with sparkling sharp spurs a large cowboy hat and a holster with two large pistols dangling from his waist. To say I felt intimidated was putting it mildly. It was like a dream come true and when I first learned I would work on *The Ed Sullivan Show*, I was so excited. However, for the first time, even though I was being noted for being a Top Ten Model, I wasn't happy, although I tried to hide it.

After the practice we broke for lunch, and an intuitive and kind Ed Sullivan came up to me. He noticed something was bothering me and asked me what was wrong. In a trembling voice and trying very hard not to break down and cry, I explained the entire episode that happened. The memory of the assault was fresh with the retelling of the details. I shuddered as I remembered the attempt to hit me with a club and strangle me, as well as being saved by the law student. I further explained how it was now impossible to feel safe living in the same apartment. I kept imagining someone was turning the doorknob. I couldn't sleep or eat and I was petrified to go back to the apartment.

Ed Sullivan was aghast. "How frightening, you have to move! You should live at the Rehearsal Club. It is a safe haven for girls in show business." He immediately had his secretary make the phone call and within minutes I was instructed to go the short distance. I learned the Rehearsal Club was at Forty-Seventh West and Fifty-Third Street, which was only a short distance from where we were working at CBS's Studio 50, on Sixth Avenue and Fifty-Third

Street. I still had time on my lunch break to meet a Mrs. Keck who was expecting me.

The Rehearsal Club was located in an old run down brownstone building. I had never heard of the place, and as I walked up the chipped front steps I reminded myself that this was not the time to be choosey. For my own mental and emotional health I had to move from the place that was a constant reminder that I had almost been murdered.

Mrs. Keck, a stout lady in her early sixties with salt-and-pepper gray hair pinned up in a bun at the back of her head, met me at the front door. We went into her office where she explained that originally the Episcopal Church had operated the Rehearsal Club as a safe haven for girls that came to New York City to perform in the arts, such as: Broadway Shows, Ballet Companies, Operas and other programs. In this way the girls would be protected and not end up on the street. Now, the Rockefeller Foundation was in charge of operating the Rehearsal Club.

It was still a safe haven and to live there a girl must have a recommendation from a priest, rabbi or minister. The recommendation from Ed Sullivan, she explained, was good enough and I was accepted. She had said that there was only room for twenty-four girls and that I was lucky, because a girl had moved out that day. Although there was a waiting list, because of the circumstances, I could move in the next day. The same morals and rules that the Francis Gill Modeling Agency had emphasized applied here, too. There could be no swearing or cussing, bikinis, "cheesecake" or belly buttons showing. In addition smoking was banned in the club! Men could not enter past the parlor door and in essence I learned The Rehearsal Club was more like a convent, I was ecstatic!

Mrs. Keck led the way up the stairs to the third floor and I followed close behind. She pointed to the buckets of sand on each landing. "There can be no cooking in your room, and ironing has to be done in the basement. In case of a fire the sand is to be used to smother it," she explained.

We entered a two-bedroom suite that I would share with two other girls. One bedroom had a single bed and I would be in the other room that had two beds. A small foyer with two closets joined the bedrooms to the bathroom. There was no shower. That meant I would have to wash my hair in the small sink with a drizzle of water. Mrs. Keck pointed to a large sponge, and said, "Each girl must scrub the tub after a bath." My bath would not be quite as glamorous as my pretend bath on *The Ed Sullivan Show*, but it would do.

A warm breeze blew in from open windows that overlooked Fifty-Third Street. *Wonderful,* I thought. *This would be a fresh beginning.* Later while living there I endured the heat as not many places in the city had air conditioners, only fans. On hot summer nights I would join some of the girls to sleep on blankets on the roof. At night a cool breeze often came across Manhattan from the East River to the Hudson River, cooling down the island.

The front part of the parlor was reserved for guests such as Abigail Rockefeller and Margaret Truman, President Harry Truman's daughter, and other Rehearsal Club Board Members when they held rummage sales for the girls. For twenty-five cents or a few dollars, the girls could buy gorgeous clothes. Later I would buy an exquisite black taffeta Christian Dior dress for only two dollars! In the back part of the parlor girls lounged in the evenings in robes and pajamas to watch and study television shows. One pay phone with no privacy hung on the wall.

In the basement, seven tables each with four chairs filled the room. In the back of the room was a kitchen with a window counter. Brunch, the only meal of the day, would be served from eleven a.m. to one p.m. A cook prepared simple items like eggs, pancakes, hamburgers, sandwiches and soup. There was no soda, only tea, coffee, milk or water.

Back in Mrs. Keck's office, I gave her twenty dollars for the first week's room and board. She gave me a key. I would move in the next day. I practically ran back to Studio 50. A dark curtain had been lifted and I would be able to get a good night's sleep. I felt as if a guardian angel had been watching over me. That day the angel, in the flesh, was Ed Sullivan. And, that night The Ed Sullivan Show was a "really gooood show," as he would say in his Irish accent. And, it certainly was!

REHEARSAL CLUB STARLETS
ESCAPADES & PERILS

O n Monday it was nearly six p.m. before I got back to the apartment. I shuddered, as I climbed the stairs. I still couldn't shake off the feeling of dread as I recalled the events of the night I was almost murdered. The evil eyes of that creep still haunted me. I offered up a quick prayer, *Thank you, God, for protecting me.*

My friend Heidi helped me carry my few belongings down to the curb. With the exception of my books, a few personal items and my clothes, I left everything else in the apartment for Heidi and her new roommate. Heidi and I knew we would keep in touch and hugged one more time as I hailed a Yellow Cab barreling down Ninth Street.

The cabbie put my belongings into the trunk of the cab and sped away keeping up with the break-neck speed of New York traffic. As we drove back up Ninth Street to Fifth Avenue, we turned north passing St. Patrick's Cathedral. I smiled to myself as I recalled happier memories, that of Confirmation the past December. I could now celebrate Mass more frequently with Bishop Fulton Sheen at the Cathedral. The Rehearsal Club was only three short blocks away from the Cathedral. In no time the cabbie stopped at the front door and helped carry my things up the chipped steps. I was grateful and gave him a small tip.

Taking a deep breath, I rang the doorbell which was opened by Mrs. Keck who greeted me warmly and cheerfully. "Welcome, the girls are anxious to meet you! One of your roommates just went upstairs." I felt I had arrived home and quickly reached for my suitcase as I started up the first flight of stairs, I would get the rest of my things later. I smiled as I passed the buckets of sand with small shovels hanging on the walls at the top of the stairs on each landing. I wondered if they had ever had a fire, at least these buckets would come in handy just in case.

I entered the suite to find my new roommate and quickly extended my hand and introduced myself, "Hi, I'm Betty, your new roommate."

"I'm Charlotte. I've been waiting to meet you. Mrs. Keck told me Ed Sullivan introduced you on his show as one of the top ten models in the country! Some of the girls and I actually saw you on the show. I can't believe it's you! And to think Tony Bennett sang to you!"

I don't know what I expected but it surely wasn't that response. This notoriety was new to me; however I quickly turned the tables as Mrs. Keck had filled me in on my roommates as well. "What about you?" I inquired. "A Rockette! That's exciting! I think Rockettes are the most famous dancers in the world, and to think you dance at Radio City Music Hall? I'm happy to meet you as well." The Radio City Music Hall was known as the most famous show place in the nation.

Charlotte laughed, "Yes, I'm thrilled to have been chosen to be a Rockette and to be working at Radio City Music Hall."

"Tell me more," I said.

She continued, "Many girls come from all over the country to try out and very few are chosen. More than six thousand people attend every show and that adds up to approximately 24,000 a day. We enjoy thunderous applause when we line up and perform our famous kicks. We are proud of the title, "Rockettes".

It was a known fact that when people visited New York City, one of the first places they enjoyed was Radio City Music Hall.

"We are world famous," Charlotte boasted, "but we work hard and make a lot of sacrifices. I came here six months ago from Pennsylvania. Right now I am doing four shows a day. I get up daily at four a.m. to rehearse for the next show and have costume fittings in between. I'm happy the Rehearsal Club is only four blocks away from Radio City since we work seven straight weeks, and then we have one week off. Even if we are only paid eighty dollars a week, being a Rockette is worth everything!"

We talked some more, and then Charlotte had to leave for the next stage performance. I learned that our other roommate, Paulette, would be in late after her performance with the New York City Ballet at Carnegie Hall. Soon Paulette would be moving out, leaving to go on tour doing shows around the country.

I put my belongings away in a small empty space in the closet. Some things I put in an empty drawer of a small bureau. Then I went down to the parlor in hopes of meeting and introducing myself to some of the other girls. Two girls were going down the block to the *Hamburger Train* to eat and invited me to join them. It was nearly eight o'clock and I had not eaten all day. I was starving, and happily accepted the invitation. I was anxious to meet new friends, and as we ate our hamburgers we got acquainted.

The *Hamburger Train* was a popular place in the show business district and was located on the corner of Sixth Avenue and Fifty-Third Street, just half a block from the Rehearsal club. Only about fifteen people at a time could be served. Everyone sat on stools at the counter. When your order was ready, the cook put it on a flatbed car of a Lionel Train, which then rolled around the counter on a track and stopped in front of you. After you took your order off the flat bed car, the train continued around the counter and back to the cook. Alex was the cook, the manager and the owner and everyone knew he loved what he was doing.

Alex always recognized new faces and introduced himself and his customers to each other. In addition he kept apprised of the latest Broadway gossip. The atmosphere there was electric! You could always count on big stars stopping in for a quick bite, the food and the atmosphere were *that* good.

Back at the Rehearsal club the parlor was filling up, as the girls were talking a-mile-a-minute to each other, catching up on the news of the day. There were girls in their pajamas and robes crowded around the television set, learning. I discovered they were most interested in learning acting and picking up on the techniques of the performers. I also noted another very popular feature of the room, and that was the line for the one telephone that was already three deep. To place a call a nickel had to be deposited into a coin slot for every three minutes. Conversations had to be short. Privacy did not exist. Everyone in the parlor could hear what you were saying, but nobody really cared. Girls who lived in the Rehearsal Club considered themselves "sisters".

Indeed, the girls who lived in the Rehearsal Club formed a "sisterhood". Since the beginning of the Club in 1913, girls had arrived from all walks of life and all parts of the country seeking a career in show business. Each girl was unique. The girls were talented, ambitious, hardworking, generous, self-sacrificing, energetic, and filled with enthusiasm. They were "ladies with good morals." Most had very little money but what little they had was spent on acting, dancing or voice lessons to improve their talents. The girls were always ready to help one another, whether by listening to a script or lending an article of clothing for a photo shoot or an interview. We cheered for each other! Sometimes we laughed together, and sometimes we cried together. We loved one another. A zest for life inspired all who lived there.

Margaret Truman and Abigail Rockefeller kept an eye on us and assisted in many ways. Once a month they held a rummage sale in the parlor collecting donated clothing from the wealthy that we could otherwise not afford. For twenty-five cents to two dollars we could buy elaborate clothing. As I shared earlier this allowed me to purchase a beautiful, designer Christian Dior dress for two dollars!

Many of the girls had problems and we shared these as well, as a sisterhood. Paulette, a ballerina, was concerned about the tendons in her upper legs being stretched out for perfect plies. It was easy to spot a professional ballerina on the streets of the city. Ballerinas always walked with their toes turned out at right angles to their bodies. After she got in bed at night she lay on her back, and put the soles of her feet together. Then one of us placed a heavy phone book on each knee. Paulette slept this way all night. Her efforts were rewarded, as she danced with the New York City Ballet for many years and toured throughout the states and Europe.

Jackie, on the other hand, had a problem with her ears sticking out. She was always tying them close to her head with a scarf that wrapped under her chin. When that didn't work, she tried gluing them to her head and managed to get her hair stuck! She even talked to a cosmetic surgeon, who surprisingly did not encourage her to undergo surgery. She could not have afforded it anyway. We reminded her that Clark Gable had the same problem and that if he could be a star, so could Jackie, even with ears sticking out! Finally, she quit worrying about her ears and she later went on to become a popular television spokeswoman.

Marie was an inspiring actress who went on dozens of interviews and try outs. She stopped by St. Patrick's Cathedral every day and prayed the rosary. Many of us helped her read scripts, but she always got turned down. She was told that she did not look the part because she was too beautiful. One night Marie came in soaking wet and her hair was a mess! Hoping to get her picture into a newspaper and be "discovered," Marie had jumped into the large fountain in Central Park. In a matter of minutes, a policeman had pulled her out of the cold water. Marie was given a police escort back to the Rehearsal Club. Marie was very depressed. She did not get any publicity, only a warning from the police officer. We all heard her crying herself to sleep that night. Then, a few nights later

Marie came home screaming with excitement. I've got a job! I've got an acting job! I changed my image!"

Marie decided to go to an interview without combing her hair or wearing makeup. A producer hired her on the spot to be one of the witches in Shakespeare's "Macbeth". The play would be performed in the evenings at the outdoor theater during the summer in Central Park. Marie was a big hit. From then on doors opened up for her.

The girls who lived in the Rehearsal Club never missed an opportunity for publicity. At Easter time, many of the girls spent hours creating elaborate hats to wear in the annual Easter Parade on Fifth Avenue in front of St. Patrick's Cathedral. Dozens of television and newspaper photographers were lined up in front of the cathedral to take pictures of those who had come from everywhere to show off their finery and elaborate Easter Bonnets. My favorite hat that one of the girls made had a birdcage on top with a real live canary inside. One girl dyed her hair lavender, and wore a lavender suit with lavender shoes. She strolled pass the photographers with a poodle that had been dyed lavender, as well. The "Easter Parade" was made popular in 1948 when Judy Garland and Fred Astaire starred in the movie by the same name.

However I felt, as a new convert that Easter was much more than parades, colored eggs, baskets and bunnies. The annual celebration of the Resurrection brings much joy to every Catholic heart. The peace of Christ dwells richly in those who meditate on His victory over sin and death. I was happy to celebrate Easter as a Catholic.

There were many famous tenants of the Rehearsal club and one was Carol Burnett, who moved out about the time I moved in. She had struggled, sacrificed, worked hard and finally made it to the big times. To us, Carol was more than that, she was a sister, made us laugh and was a genuine comedian and best of all, our heroine! We watched her on *The Gary Moore Show*, and other television appearances. Carol Burnett inspired us.

When one of my roommates Paulette moved out, to travel with the New York City Ballet, another girl moved in, named Doris

Smith. But she quickly changed her name to Doris Bourgeois. She was a past "Miss New Orleans," with a thick southern accent, dancing, crystal blue eyes and dozens of blond curls that framed her beautiful smiling face. Doris had won a hot pepper eating contest with the grand prize a trip to New York City to try out for show business. Doris would soon change her name again and this time to Tina Baron. The girls shared clothes with her when she went on interviews. Tina wore my red sweater almost as much as I did. Tina had a problem with biting her nails. We convinced her that she had to let her nails grow out and suggested that she eat lots of Jell-O. Instead, she poured a packet of dry gelatin into her mouth every day. It caked on her teeth before it dissolved. We laughed at her antics but the result was that Tina finally grew beautiful nails.

I was one of the girls that helped her practice a script from the movie, "Picnic." She eventually passed her screen tests and moved to Hollywood, California. She changed her name yet again. This time her name was Donna Douglas who became the well-known character of Ellie Mae Clampett on the hit television show of the sixties, "The Beverly Hillbillies." There often was a mystery surrounding Donna. Sometimes, while living at the Rehearsal Club, she received large bunches of red roses. Often we saw her sitting on her bed, holding the roses and crying. We left her to her privacy. The last time I saw Donna was in the 1980's in Wauchula, Florida. She was in a Bible ministry and Donna gave her testimony on being a Christian, and sang songs for the audience who loved her, bought her tapes and lined up for autographs.

I was last in touch with Donna in 2013 and 2014 when she gave me permission to include her in the Rehearsal Club Memoirs for the 100th Anniversary. I cherish the autographed photo she sent me. Donna never shared she was ill, and when I learned she passed away on New Year's Day in 2015, I cried. Donna survived the industry with "good morals" and will be remembered not just as a roommate in the Rehearsal Club, but her love for Jesus and her love and kindness to others.

Another "sister," Vicky Martin was a professional singer who performed with Edie Adams on the *Ernie Kovacs Show*. Vicky also sang with the Frank Silver's Band. Frank Silver and Irving Cohn were famous for the song they wrote which sold over two million copies, "Yes, We have No Bananas." When Vicky and Frank began a serious relationship, Vicky sometimes came back to the club and found bananas piled on her bed. Eventually, Vicky and Frank married. Tragically he passed away when she was pregnant with their son, Frank.

Vicky and I developed a lifelong friendship; she never remarried. Our children grew up playing together in Central Park. She had a deep devotion to St. Jude. When she visited me after I moved to Florida, we often formed a rosary with seashells in the sand on the beach, and as the sun set, prayed with our children. Vicky lived in Jersey City and was responsible for many Marian and Pro-Life Activities. She was an inspirational Godmother to my third child.

The list goes on and on of the personalities who made the Rehearsal Club famous: Sandy Duncan, Lucille Ball, Blythe Danner, Carol Burnette, Donna Douglas, Denise Pence, Rise Clemmer, Dottie Belle and the Rockettes, and the Ziegfeld girls, just to name a few. In 2013 the Rehearsal Club celebrated a Centennial. I joined many of the other former residents, in New York City for the festivities. One of the highlights was a real Broadway Production put on by the past residents called "Good Girls Only." Blythe Danner gave us a party at the famous Sardi's Restaurant and Carol Burnette gave us a party at the Players Club. Indeed, it is an honor to have lived at the Rehearsal Club where manners and morals were as important as talent.

Show business was not only fun for me but at times hazardous. Because I was considered versatile, I could be posing for *Vogue* one minute, climbing rocks in Central Park while posing for *Seventeen Magazine,* or making jelly for a *Good House Keeping Magazine*. I was in demand for television commercials and fashion shows. I traveled extensively for over four years for Metro Golden Mayer filming "Fashions in the News," that was shown in movie theaters throughout the country. I reigned as "Queen of the Diamond Industry," in New York, "Queen of the National Boat Show," and appeared with Ethel Merman as "Queen of the National Business Show," at the Coliseum. Traveling opened up my mind and heart to many parts of the world and a desire to share the love of the risen Man on the cross, Jesus.

At times it wasn't always so glamorous. One time, machine gun fire rang out as I quickly sprang out of bed and ran to the window to see what was happening. Six flights below on the lawn of the International Hotel in the Dominican Republic soldiers and civilians chased one another, firing guns. Several civilians fell to the ground, as we watched. Several minutes later a soldier pounded on the door of our room. The other models and I were too scared to open the door. The pounding continued. Finally, when we opened it, a soldier in a broken-English demanded somewhat stiltedly, "American Party pick up at two o'clock and go to the stadium. You will sit with Rafael Trujillo and watch a parade."

I was one of four American Models, joined by a photographer, a representative from Eileen Sportswear, and the advertisement manager who had come to the Dominican Republic for a filming of the latest spring fashions. We had been there three days and had enjoyed the hotel and lavish accommodations. Later when the other models and I floated down a waterway in a small boat for a photo shoot, we saw a different side to the Dominican Republic. On the banks of the water, hundreds of poor, starving people stood staring at us. Some had cardboard boxes for shelter. Most had nothing to shield them from the heat or rain. Most had inflated bellies and skeletal bones showing underneath the skin. I was nauseated.

Sure enough at two p.m. another two soldiers with guns on their shoulders arrived. We were really frightened as we were ushered and then driven to the stadium in a black limousine. We were ordered to mount the steps to the top of a grandstand and sit next to Rafael Trujillo, one of the cruelest dictators to ever walk the earth. Trujillo was later assassinated in 1961.

We watched as every man, woman, and child that lived in the Dominican Republic was made to process past him, raise an arm, and shout, "Hail, Trujillo!" or face harsh punishment. We were then driven back to the hotel with an invitation for later that evening. Our group was ordered to attend a dinner party at Trujillo's home and again a driver was dispatched to pick us up in the black limousine where we were escorted through an iron gate where a dozen soldiers pointed guns with bayonets at us. Inside his home, I was so nervous and shaking, I threw up!

Trujillo approached me. "Are you sick?" he demanded. When I nodded my head, he said in a rough voice, "One of my men will drive you back to the hotel!"

Later after I was driven back to the hotel, I nearly panicked thinking what could have happened to me. I anxiously waited and prayed for the rest of our group. Finally, they returned. We had been warned that the entire hotel was bugged and not to say anything at all.

The next morning Trujillo's soldiers whisked us off to the airport. A plane was waiting. During the entire time I had been in the Dominican Republic, I had not seen one church, priest, or a clergy of any denomination, crucifix, or joy among the people. I was very disheartened. As our plane landed back in New York, the Statue of Liberty never looked so beautiful to me!

Another time, Young and Rubican, an advertising agency, held a promotion for Piels Beer, one of their clients. An island in the Bahamas would be the grand prize. To assure the public it was beautiful, as well as livable, I was one of the three models selected to be dropped off on the island and left for three days. A female reporter from CBS would be with us to record our comments. A photographer and an ad agent would also round out the group. Our party was flown from New York to Nassau in the Bahamas. Then we were flown by seaplane to an uninhibited island that was in the middle of nowhere. We wore sneakers as we jumped out of the seaplane into the water because we were told beds of sharp coral would cut our feet. We kicked nurse sharks away, as we made our way to the beach. The pilot dropped off our supplies and flew back to Nassau. He left drinking water, but unfortunately, he forgot to leave our food. There was no way for us to communicate beyond the island. Cell phones, iPads and computers were yet to be invented!

Standing in the center of the island, we could see all of it. Fortunately, the girl from CBS discovered a bed of live conch on the west side of the island. Raw conch is all we had to eat for the next three days. We used machetes to hack out huts from thick bushes to get out of the sun. At night we slept in netted hammocks. Scorpions with their curved tails high in the air scurried everywhere. We cheered when the seaplane returned. We had survived, and now we could eat real cooked food. However, before retiring to a hotel in Nassau, we had to be in another publicity shot. As we sped through crystal blue water in a small motorboat with fish tied to the back end we soon noticed that sharks were chasing us! We didn't need to be told to keep our hands in the boat!

Back in New York City, as part of the publicity for Piels Beer, a barge had been decorated as an island. For the next two weeks the other two models and I dressed in sarongs and fed grapes to Dave Galloway, the first host of the *Today Show*, as he broadcasted live from the barge, while we floated around the Island of Manhattan. The media had a heyday with publicity. Newsweek even printed a photo of the floating island in their magazine.

Onward to the streets of Paris, France where I was shocked to see latrines on the sidewalks and unisex restrooms featuring open holes on the floors. The lack of refrigeration for dead chickens displayed for sale atop wooden boxes in front of delicatessens cautioned me to be mindful of what I ate. Bullet riddled buildings gave me compassion and sympathy for the people of Paris. They were our Allies, bravely fighting alongside the United States. While World War II had ended, by the signs of the times, the people were still recuperating.

After posing for photos all day in Paris, I was invited to see the famous "Can-Can Girls" show, but when I learned it also featured nude dancing, I declined. There was somewhere else I knew I would rather be. I climbed the hill of Montmartre and found Jesus waiting for me in the Blessed Sacrament of the Basilica of the Sacred Heart. Earlier that day during a photo shoot at Montmartre, I learned that perpetual adoration of the Blessed Sacrament had been going on there for many years. Knowing that Jesus is always waiting for me and I could find Him present, Body, Blood, Soul and Divinity, in France was no comparison to a show, no matter how famous. Nothing else could fill me with the warmth of His love.

Another time, flying over Normandy and en route for a photo shoot in London, I saw the beach where there were many white crosses signifying the loss of life and bomb craters. I saw the bullet holes on Winston Churchill's home. All were reminders of why I had cried myself to sleep during the years of World War II. When all of mankind turns to Jesus, the risen Man on the cross, there will be peace.

Back in New York a seemingly uneventful fashion show became newsworthy. When I mounted a very high-tiered runway for a fashion show at the famous Waldorf Astoria, I was carrying a large bouquet of yellow pom-poms that I was to throw out into the audience. When I reached the top of the runway, spotlights glared and I was blinded. I couldn't see anything. I tossed out the pom-poms and then I heard a terrifying loud crash! Apparently, the bouquet hit a waiter causing him to drop a tray of dishes. There was a thunderous roar of laughter and applause. I couldn't even see how to come down the steps. So, I just stood at the top the tier and shook with laughter, too. Surprisingly I didn't get fired! My agent loved the publicity.

KNIGHT IN SHINING ARMOUR

Charlotte flew up the stairs and burst into our room. Breathlessly, she exclaimed, "Leon Leonidoff is interviewing high fashion models to perform with the Rockettes at Radio City Music Hall. The silk industry wants fashion models to wear elaborate gowns and be part of the show. The interviews are tomorrow morning at ten o'clock. Betty, you have *got to go*! I know you'll be picked! It will be fun! You'll love being on that stage and hearing the thunderous applause from over 6,000 people at every show."

Leon Leonidoff was the most famous producer and choreographer in the world. He created the shows at Radio City Music Hall for forty-two years. To work with him would be a thrill of a lifetime. Then I wondered what my modeling agent, Francis Gill and my television-film agents, Swartz and Luskin, would say. I was on contract with them for a lot more money than I would be getting at Radio City Music Hall. I also had to think of my cancer research projects at New York University. I decided to go for the interview without telling my agents or my director at the University. Maybe I wouldn't even be chosen!

The next morning I was one of dozens of girls lined up to be interviewed. Leon Leonidoff flipped through my portfolio of pictures and resumes, and then he surprised me by asking, "Do I recognize you from *The Ed Sullivan Show*? Did he introduce you as one of the top ten models in the country?"

"Yes, he did. Tony Bennett sang to me," I answered.

He asked me to walk across the stage as if I was modeling an evening gown. I was hired on the spot. I had to sign a contract that I would be at four shows a day for twelve weeks and that my stage makeup would be exactly the same as the Rockettes. No one in the audience should be able to pick out anyone on stage. Even the *Corp de Ballet* girls had to makeup their faces as the Rockettes.

Ten models had been chosen. Our gowns were to be furnished by the Silk Industry. Each model was given two gowns to wear, one for the opening of the stage show and one to be worn at the finale, as we danced and modeled with the dancing Rockettes. Both of my gowns were exquisite! My favorite gown that I would be modeling was an original from Nelly de Grab. It was strapless. The skirt ballooned out with large panels of red and black silk. The dress looked like something that could be worn on stage by a "Can-Can" dancer in Paris. I was told it was worth $3,000! The headpiece, a Lily Dache original and made of black velvet with a protruding flower, was worth $200! The other dress was also strapless and made of panels and panels of flowing pink silk.

The stage show started with the models standing on the staircases on the sidewalls of the massive theater. We slowly danced down the stairs to the stage. This was scary! The stairs were narrow and high. If anyone slipped or tripped, she would land far below in someone's lap! Once we were on stage, we walked out on a very long runway that was over the orchestra pit and the first three rows of the theater and showed off our gowns. Each model had her own spotlight on her, the entire time.

While the show went on with more performers, we changed into our other gowns and reappeared with the *Corp de Ballet*. Then, the Rockettes joined us for the finale. They always brought the house down with a thunderous applause, as they lined up and did their famous kicks.

As I suspected, my agents were not happy about my being tied up for twelve weeks and for so little money. However, they understood other doors would be opened for me by this exposure. The director at the University Cancer Lab gave me his blessing, too. Since the show would be starting in June, and the lab would be closed most of the summer, there would be no conflict with my cancer research.

Back at the Rehearsal Club the Rockettes who lived there were as excited as I was that I had been picked. I thanked Charlotte over and over for telling me about the interview. I couldn't believe it! Everything about Radio City Music Hall was spectacular with more than 6,000 seats, the fabulous Wurlitzer Organ which had 4,410 pipes and was by far the largest theater organ in the world, and even the location, in the middle of Rockefeller Plaza. The movie, "Houseboat", would be shown in between the stage shows. Sophia Loren and Cary Grant, the stars of the movie, would be visiting us backstage. When I did meet them, Cary Grant was incredibly handsome, and Sophia Loren was tiny, but beautiful.

June 25, 1958 could not come too soon. Waiting for the first day of the show was like waiting for Christmas. Little did I know what else would be in store for me that day!

I slid onto a stool and ordered my favorite breakfast at the Hamburger Train—a glazed doughnut and a cup of coffee. Suddenly, I became acutely aware of an energy flowing from someone sitting on the stool next to me. When Alex introduced us to each other, I turned to look at the man. My heart skipped a beat and I nearly swooned. His dazzling eyes seemed to penetrate deeply into my soul. I wanted to stroke his massive black hair and gently touch his mustache to see if he were real. His contagious smile with those beautiful white teeth set me on fire. *What was happening? I had heard of love at first sight. Was this it?*

His name was Phil Galvano. When I got ready to leave, Phil unexpectedly paid for my breakfast and for the coffee and doughnuts that I was taking back to my roommates at the Rehearsal Club. I knew the girls would be happy to have a free breakfast. Before we parted, Phil asked me if he could call me some time. Not wanting to be rude, I nervously told him he could. *Was Phil feeling what I was feeling? Would he call me?*

Two minutes later, I walked into the Rehearsal Club. The one phone in the Rehearsal Club was ringing. "Betty, it's for you!" someone shouted.

I went to the phone and couldn't believe it! It was Phil who asked, "May I take you out to dinner tonight?" My heart raced as I explained that I would be performing in four shows that day at Radio City Music Hall and that I would not be free until ten p.m. "Fine," he answered. "I'll be waiting for you at the stage door."

The first show began at noon. My face looked just like every other model and Rockette. It was a requirement of Leon Leonidoff, the producer and choreographer that everyone's face looked the same from the audience's point-of-view. This was to keep people in the audience from calling out to their friends. We wore very heavy make-up, black eyeliner and mascara.

When the music began all of the models were in place on the staircases and slowly began to dance down the steps. I was at the top of the staircase, which was high and I was nervous. *Dear God,* I prayed, *please don't let any of us trip.* Once I was on stage, I was not fearful. I was comfortable on runways and the rest of the show went well.

After the last performance, the models gathered in the fourth floor dressing room to change clothes, remove the stage makeup and talk about the day. Some of the girls went to a window to see if their dates had arrived at the stage door.

"Wow! Whose date is that?" the girls cried out.

I was sitting in front of a mirror removing heavy mascara. I jumped up and ran to the window. I looked down at the stage door, and my mouth fell open. There was Phil like a knight in shining armor! Phil with his massive black hair and his black mustache was stunning in a white silk suit with a red rose in his lapel. Instead of sitting on a horse, he was sitting in a silver Eldorado Convertible.

From my vantage point the convertible looked twice as long as it really was.

"No, no, no!" I cried out. "I can't go out with him! He looks like a smoothie! I'm scared of him, please, one of you take my place. Someone go down and tell him I got sick. I'll go out the other stage door. He makes me nervous!" I cried out.

No one volunteered to take my place and I was stuck. If only they knew that deep down I really wanted to keep the date with Phil. I had never met anyone who had filled me with so much excitement and made me so nervous, at the same time. Yes, I was scared of him, but I wondered, *Am I in love?*

Phil greeted me with a warm smile. My heart leaped again. He was handsome and charming. Phil opened the car door for me, and I got in. He slid in on the other side. Before driving off, he gave me a little bag with ribbons tied around it. Phil watched me, as I untied the ribbons and looked inside. Dark Red Bing Cherries!

"I heard they are your favorite," he said with a twinkle in his eyes.

"Oh, yes, they certainly are!" I exclaimed. "Thank you for being so thoughtful!" I later learned that he asked a friend who shared this information with him.

We drove to a nearby Chinese restaurant for dinner. A waiter pulled out the table from the wall so we could sit beside each other on the leather seat. After the waiter pushed the table back, Phil picked up my hand. I felt electricity shoot through every fiber of my body. *Was I about to die?* I was too nervous to look at him.

Phil ordered a special lobster dish, fried rice and chicken chow mein. I marveled at the way he skillfully mixed the lobster sauce and fried rice together, and then, served the food to our plates. His manners were impeccable.

After dinner Phil suggested that we take a drive around Manhattan. The weather was warm and balmy. He drove us in the convertible with the top down. Skyscrapers were lit up and the stars were bright and clear. Driving along the East River on the east side of the island, we took deep breaths inhaling the salty air.

Soon we were on Riverside Drive on the west side of the island. Phil pulled into a parking area near the George Washington Bridge that was well lit. Other people were parked there, too. Across the Hudson River, the Palisades Amusement Park lit up the shore with big Ferris wheels, a roller coaster and merry-go-rounds. Lighted boats floated up and down the river. This was a very romantic place to just sit and talk.

Then, Phil got out of the car and he went to the trunk. I began to shake like a leaf. *What was he doing? Why didn't I just tell Phil to take me home after dinner? Why was I nervous when I loved every minute of the evening?* Phil soon came back. He had gotten his ukulele. I stopped shaking.

Phil played his ukulele, and sang love songs to me. He sang beautiful Italian love songs! As he sang every word with emotion, he looked deep into my eyes. Italians are known to do everything with feeling. They cry hard, they laugh hard and they love deeply. Then, he was singing "Tear a wing from a bird and he can't fly..." Phil suddenly sounded so sad. He was opening his soul to me. At that moment I knew his soul had met my soul. I knew I loved him and somehow I knew that Phil loved me. I knew I wanted to spend the rest of my life with Phil. We had just met, but it was as though we had known each other from the beginning of time. *How could this be?*

A policeman on duty at the rest area strolled over to where we were. "I sure have been enjoying the music," he said. "Can you play "Five Foot Two, Eyes of Blue?"

Phil played the tune while the policeman tapped his fingers on the hood of the car. We soon left realizing that it was nearly 1:00 a.m., and as he drove me home we passed St. Patrick's Cathedral. I noticed Phil made the sign of the cross, as he had done earlier when we passed the church coming this same way. Additionally, I noticed the St. Christopher's Medal on the dashboard, and medals on a chain around his neck. He was Catholic! Thank you, God!

After leaving the car in a parking garage, Phil and I walked two blocks to the Rehearsal Club. I wondered if he would kiss me, but

Phil, only said, "Goodnight," and then, "I will pick you up at the same time tomorrow night."

I was dumbfounded. *Was he taking me for granted?* In the South where I grew up, a gentleman always, politely asked, "May I see you again?"

Breaking Southern protocol, I agreed and said, "Yes."

I then learned Phil lived across the street. His apartment was on the fourth floor. My room was on the third floor. We could actually spy on each other. *Was this a good thing? I knew we would both be keeping the drapes closed.*

However, my roommates began waking me up when they saw Phil leaving his apartment building in the mornings. I would throw a scarf over my head and pull on a trench coat, saunter into the Hamburger Train, and act surprised to see Phil. I'd have coffee with him and then he would offer to pay for the coffee and doughnuts I always took back to the girls. It was a little bit of a racket! Phil was amused, but understood the girls were struggling to work and spent their extra money on classes. Besides, seeing Phil often was wonderful for us both, because I knew we were in love!

UNITED IN LOVE

I t was evident to everyone that Phil and I had fallen madly in love with each other. Although both of us were extremely busy, Phil with his television appearances, writing assignments and teaching golf lessons. I took classes, grew cancer cells, and helped students in the microbiology classes at the University, and modeled. Our days were not complete without spending as much time as we could together.

In late summer my modeling agent booked me on an assignment to be shot in Maine. Although I did not smoke and never did, because my mother had taught me that ladies do not smoke, an advertising representative for Chesterfield Cigarettes requested that I be photographed lobster fishing for an advertising campaign. I would not have to hold a cigarette or smoke. The assignment would take two days.

Phil said he could not bear the thought of my being gone so long. I told him I did not want to be away from him either, but I needed to go because I needed to support myself, and my modeling agent would be upset if I didn't. Doing the shoot for Chesterfield Cigarettes would pay me $200 a day, which was a top price in those days. Reluctantly, Phil agreed.

Early one morning the photographer, the Chesterfield ad agent and I left for Maine in an overloaded station wagon. Late afternoon we arrived at a tiny resort town in Maine that had all but closed up for the summer. A woman who operated a bed and breakfast where we were to stay had been waiting for us. She gave us a hearty welcome. Her husband had already left for Florida where they ran another bed and breakfast in the winter. The ad agent had paid her to stay behind, to house and feed us for the two days while I was photographed lobster fishing for the promotion.

Well, guess what? The sky turned dark gray, the wind became fierce. Rain pounded the tin roof of the home. The local lobster fishermen who would be shooting scenes with me informed us that lobster fishing is only done under a bright blue sky. The local weatherman reported the weather would be the same for the next three days. The shooting would have to be postponed until then.

The ad agent was determined to shoot the scenes before going back to New York and that he would not leave. He convinced the woman who ran the bed and breakfast to stay open the extra days. He would pay her double. The only problem she said, was that all the stores but a drugstore in town had closed for the season. The only thing left in her freezer for us to eat were lobsters! However, eggs, butter, and bread could be bought at the local drugstore.

Three days slowly turned into six days. The ad agent and photographer sat glued to a card table in the lounge playing gin rummy. I found a hoola hoop in the parlor and spent a lot of time perfecting the exercise in the privacy of my room. The three of us got together to eat lobsters twice a day! Occasionally we took walks in the rain and speculated about the weather. Television did not exist in the resort town. Computers or cell phones had not come into use. Electricity failed off and on because of the storm. Kerosene lamps sat out in the parlor.

Many phone lines had blown down. When the switchboard operator finally got Phil and me connected by phone, Phil was beside himself. He blurted out, "Six days! I can't stand it! As soon as you get back to the city, we are getting married!"

What a cute way to say he misses me or was this proposal? I thought. After all, I had not even thought of getting married, yet. Although I knew I loved him, somewhere in the back of my mind, I was still considering becoming a doctor.

After six days, the rain and wind stopped. The sky turned bright blue. I donned a bright yellow rain slicker and yellow rain hat for the shooting. Our crew went to a dock where a dozen fishermen were dressed just like me and were hauling in traps full of lobsters. As directed I stood in the middle of the fishermen taking lobsters out of traps. I pretended to help them, as I held up squirming lobsters while being extra careful not to be pinched by one. The photographer shot dozens and dozens of scenes. The shooting was finally over. The ad agent was satisfied. Later some of the shots would be seen on big billboards bordering highways, posters on walls in stores and pages in magazines.

As soon as we got back to the city, and I had been dropped off with my luggage at the Rehearsal Club, I practically ran the five blocks to the golf academy. As soon as I got off the elevator on the second floor, and stepped into the waiting room, Phil saw me. He was giving a golf lesson to young man in one of the golf cages. He immediately stopped the lesson. He told his pupil the lesson was over and to come back the next day for a free lesson. The man was very pleased!

Phil then took me by the hand. We went down the elevator and walked out of the building and down the block. Phil was grinning with a twinkle in his eyes. *What in the world I thought.* I had no idea where he was leading me. The next thing I knew he was taking me into a doctor's office. I heard him tell the receptionist we needed to get Wasserman tests. I had never heard of the tests. Later I would find out the State of New York required all people getting married to have the tests.

After the tests were over, we walked into the popular Shraft's Restaurant for a cup of coffee. Who was sitting there having coffee, too? Ed Sullivan and one of his assistants! We greeted one another. I knew Ed because I had worked with him on some of his television shows. He knew Phil, because of his television show and because he took golf lessons from him. Phil broke the news that we were getting married! Well, Ed's column in the *Daily News* was one of the most popular and most read pieces in all of Manhattan. Ed wrote in his column, which appeared the very next day, that Phil and I had just gotten back from Bermuda where we were on our honeymoon! Of course, this was not true!

Now people all over Manhattan, the show business world, the golfing world and my colleagues at New York University were calling to congratulate us. Nick Kenny and other gossip columns in other newspapers ran the news, too. After all, Phil had been considered one of the most eligible bachelors on Broadway. We were in a pickle! We did not want to tell anyone that we were not married, but that we would be getting married. We needed to keep our mouths shuts. The gossip columns would only make things worse. We needed to work things out with the Church. We decided to let people think we were indeed married, although I still lived across the street from him in the Rehearsal Club. This was another problem. The girls at the club were perplexed. Why was I married and had not moved across the street to live with Phil? To make things more confusing, I was wearing a wedding band. Phil had surprised me by giving me a handcrafted gold wedding band. While I was in Maine, he had designed it with a friend who worked in the jewelry district in Manhattan. We decided I should wear it now, since we were pretending to be married and people would want to see my ring.

I did not have a diamond and never would. The reason being that in my social circle, diamonds were a status symbol and I was never materialistic. In fact, Phil often walked me past Tiffany's to look in the showroom window and all I could comment on was the cute, ceramic bunnies that held the diamonds—part of the display. I learned later that Phil thought I was joking. He verified with a friend that diamonds were just not that important to me. The wedding band was wide enough to prevent me from wearing another ring.

The publicity was all so confusing, and we wanted to keep our privacy! We avoided everyone we could. Father Butler was amused, but helped us do the right thing. Our wedding day was bittersweet. We had a very private ceremony with two witnesses. Although Phil's family had welcomed me into their lives with open arms, no one from my family welcomed Phil or wished us happiness. I not only hurt for myself, but for Phil, who truly wanted to be part of my family, too. He was Catholic and that was the biggest problem for my family to accept. There had been a shimmer of hope by my family, especially by my grandmother, that someday I would come to my senses and abandon the Catholic faith. I knew this would never happen. Jesus had brought me to the Catholic faith. I loved Him, and I was His.

The wedding took place on a Saturday. Phil and I were deliriously happy to at last be united as one. After the ceremony we drove to the Lakewood Country Club in Lakewood, New Jersey. As a wedding present, Phil gave me a golf bag with a set of Kenneth Smith golf clubs. Phil thought it would be fun for me to play my first round of golf on our wedding day! While most people might think this is horrible, I loved it, and I loved him. Seriously, since the wedding was so unplanned, he and I both had commitments to keep. He was still taping his golf show, and I was taping commercials. Later on, we did have a honeymoon.

Phil must have been in love, because he sure had extra patience that day, since I knew nothing about golf course etiquette and I shot 168! He shot sixty-nine which was three under par. Thanks to Phil who was known as the best golf teacher in the world, within six months I would be shooting golf in the 70's and playing tournaments with the Metropolitan Ladies Golf Association.

Later that day some of the girls who lived in the Rehearsal Club congratulated us, and they helped us move my few items across the street to Phil's apartment. The apartment was typical Italian and very masculine with white walls, trimmed with black woodwork and red drapes and leather furniture. That night Phil asked me if there was anything I wished I could have someday. I answered that

I would like to have a big table with lots of guests to serve. Little did I realize that my wish would come true. Through the years our table would always be full with many guests and our own six children, a great blessing!

Phil was pleasantly surprised that I knew so much about cooking. He could now have home-cooked meals. Most New Yorkers eat out a lot in restaurants and delicatessens. My cooking skills had been honed, as I grew up during World War II. If we did not grow it, we could not eat it! Only staples like flour, salt and cornmeal could be bought at a local grocery store. There were no restaurants in Conover! I had made my first biscuits at five years old. I dearly loved to cook and soon learned recipes of all of his favorite Italian dishes from members of his family. Phil always praised my cooking even once when I burned toast. His gratitude made me strive to be the best cook I could.

When Phil learned I had plucked and dressed as many as twenty-five chickens in one morning back home in North Carolina, he was ecstatic! Phil loved to go duck or pheasant hunting with friends in New Jersey, but he did not know how to dress the poultry or prepare it for cooking. I did. During hunting seasons he came home to the small apartment with a burlap sack containing his bounties. Sometimes after I had plucked and dressed the birds, feathers could be found throughout the apartment, but dinner was fantastic! Phil was always pleased for guests to share the feast.

Most New York apartments did not have freezers. Microwave ovens were for the future. Air conditioners were a novelty. To get cool in the evenings, we sometimes climbed an iron ladder to the roof where other tenants were cooling off and enjoying a sea breeze. One of Phil's pupils offered him a deal he could not refuse. The pupil asked Phil to trade golf lessons for an air conditioner. Phil agreed and a window unit was installed in our two-room apartment. A tube holding the wiring was attached down the side of the building to a box for electricity. We were amazed and delighted that the apartment got cool. Many curious visitors checked out this new commodity!

Bill Mote was one of the most interesting and fascinating pupils Phil ever had. Back in Florida, Bill and his partner, Ted Bartels, as teenagers owned a pickup truck and made local deliveries. They eventually came to New York and worked at the shipping docks in lower Manhattan. Bill came up with the idea of using a conveyor belt to move freight trailers already loaded back, and forth from trucks to train flatbeds. This made transportation quicker and more economical. His invention revolutionized the transportation industry in the United States and Europe. Eventually he owned Republic Carloading, and Yale Trucking and half of Southern Railway.

We often spent time with Bill and his wife, Lenore, at their estate in Westchester, New York. Bill owned a complex of apartments on Anna Maria Island in Florida, where he sent his clients and friends to vacation. Phil and I were invited to have a belated honeymoon there in March. The pristine beaches with white sand and crystal blue water made it one of the most beautiful places we had ever seen. Golfing was great! We bought a small cottage while we were there. That began our connection to Florida.

Bill held the record for catching the world's largest fish, a marlin, caught off the coast of Peru. Phil and I joined Bill and Lenore on Broadway at Times Square for the World Premier of Hemmingway's "Old Man in the Sea" starring Spencer Tracy and featuring the fish Bill had caught! The Mote Marine Laboratory and Aquarium on Longboat Key is another tribute to Bill.

I ended up resigning and putting my education on hold after I married Phil but still modeled a while longer. I was a certified tissue-culturist and had been working on my undergraduate and master's degree at the same time—with special permission. While I was sad to see that part of my life end, I was excited about what the future held.

On February 9, 1961, one of the worst snowstorms to ever hit New York City caused traffic to come to a standstill. Three feet of snow blanketed the streets. Narrow paths for pedestrians were dug down the middle of the streets, even Fifth Avenue. All cars, taxicabs, buses and other vehicles were banned from the city. About three a.m. I began to feel a little strange. Contractions alerted me that our firstborn was about to arrive, horror of horrors! There was no one, not even a policeman to escort us. We had no choice. We walked eight long blocks to the Polyclinic Hospital in snow and ice, and prayed all the way. We barely made it! We thanked God that our doctor had been stranded at the hospital and would have to spend the night there. Philip Peter was born at 5:30 in the morning.

Later my Jewish doctor shared with me that he had never seen a man so happy and cry so much over a newborn baby. He said babies are not only great treasures, but Jewish tradition says they are born with a loaf of bread and many blessings. This was true in our case as well. Phil made a large sale of golf clubs that morning and Philip came to us with many blessings of joy that have lasted through the years. Life took on a new meaning.

We were flooded with phone calls and visitors. The news media filled gossip columns, television and radio shows of the news of Philip's birth. Phil even hung an oversized banner on Fifth Avenue from the second floor, golf academy that proclaimed, "It's a boy!"

Fifteen months later God blessed us with Elizabeth Rose, another little miracle. She was beautiful with dark hair and long dainty fingers. Occasionally, Philip and Elizabeth modeled with me in family settings for television and magazines, but that soon stopped. Instead we played in Central Park, rode the merry-go-round and wandered through the Museum of Natural History. Nothing had become more important or more fun than being the best wife and mother I could be. I rejoiced every moment of everyday.

Phil was happy with whatever decision I made, however we were still in the thick of things. We were invited to many premiers and special events—so while I was no longer modeling, I still enjoyed much of the social scene; more importantly with Phil and my young family.

Philip and Elizabeth were both baptized at Saint Patrick's Cathedral. Every Sunday we could be found sitting near the sanctuary. I wanted the children to see what was going on.

Sometimes services were like Broadway Productions with the Knights of Columbus and the priests. One morning as the procession left the sanctuary at the end of Mass, Bishop Fulton J. Sheen stopped in front of Philip and Elizabeth. Then with his piercing and dancing eyes he waited until he had their full attention. He then raised his hand and blessed each child with the sign of the cross. What a wonderful blessing.

This incident brought to mind a time before I had even met Phil. I was standing with a crowd on a street corner waiting for a light to change. I had just come from a shooting for Vogue. I was still wearing heavy makeup. I felt a penetrating stare from someone. I turned to see Bishop Sheen! He did not speak to me in words, but by the look he gave me, I knew he was praying for me. Surely, he knew how easy it is for models to go astray. I have been praying for Fulton J Sheen, as he is on the road to sainthood.

FILIPO SANTO GALVANO

ilipo Santo Galvano (Philip Saint Galvano) was born on East Eleventh Street on lower Manhattan on All Saints Day, November 1, 1915. The midwife who delivered him in the meager place the immigrant family called home declared him dead. Mama Rosa cried out in pain and agony, "No! No! Blessed Mother let him live!"

The midwife reluctantly picked up the pathetic looking infant again. Holding him firmly by his ankles, she gave him another strong smack across his rear. Gasping, the infant let out a startling cry. Mama Rosa smiled a sigh of relief. She always relied heavily on prayers she offered to Mary, the Mother of Jesus. As a matter of fact the rosary never left her hands.

Pietro Galvano had come to the United States in 1908. A few months earlier than Rosa, now docked with their eight children in the shadow of the Statue of Liberty at Ellis Island in 1909. Rosa's father had been the President of the House of Congress in Palermo, Sicily. Pietro had been a soldier. They came to America, the land of opportunity, seeking a better life.

In the beginning the family was homeless. They found space to live with relatives who had migrated earlier and lived in Brooklyn. Papa Pietro worked as a chef, and eventually opened his own restaurant, the Rex. Times were tough for many years to come. When Phil was five years old, he stood on a box and washed dishes in the restaurant. He often made trips to a coat factory and brought coats home for Mama Rosa to make buttonholes on them. Then, he would take them back to the factory and pick up more coats. When Phil was eight years old he canvassed the neighborhood selling vanilla. At nine years old he was making leather belts in a factory.

There was no electricity in the neighborhood where they lived. They were glad when winter came, so the fire escape could be used for a refrigerator. Water had to be carried up the stairs to the fourth floor. For a nickel, baths were available on Saturday evenings down the street. The only toy Phil could ever remember owning was a skate he found, from which he made a skateboard.

At ten years old Phil became a caddy at a local golf course. This is when he fell in love with golf. His first golf club was a rock tied to a stick. While everyone was telling him to put that stick down and do something worthwhile, little did they know the impact that golf club would have on his life someday.

After serving in the Army Air Corp during World War II, Phil returned to New York City and to his childhood passion, golf. Eventually, the *Galvano Golf Academy* was located on Fifth Avenue across from *Tiffany's*. Every celebrity of television, Broadway or movies, interested in golf knew about or visited the golf academy. Phil was billed as the foremost golf instructor in the world. People from all over the world flew to New York for lessons. Phil wrote four books on golf. One made the New York Times Bestsellers list and the praise of President Eisenhower, who read the book while recuperating from his heart attack.

In 1954, executives from the Du Mont WABD Television Company which became NBC, told Phil that they did not think there was an audience for golf, but asked if he would be willing to try a show for twenty-six weeks. Television broadcasts were done live in those days, known as the Golden Age of television. No taping and replays. Phil's show ran for twenty-six weeks and was a smash hit. Bishop Fulton Sheen's award winning show, *Life is*

Worth Living, ran back to back with the golf show. Bishop Sheen and Phil even became good friends. Bishop Sheen used to say as soon as he got too old for tennis he would take up golf.

Phil knew many famous people that frequented his golf academy including: Perry Como, Frankie Laine, and Ed Sullivan who were all professed Catholics; Robert Merrill, Joey Bishop, Willie Mosconi the billiard champion (and fifteen times World Champion) who would become Godfather to one of our sons; Jackie Gleason, Morey Amsterdam (Phil was Godfather to his son, Greg); Johnny Carson (who we often doubled dated with); Dinah Shore, Betty Grable; Carol Lawrence and Robert Goulette who used to meet secretly at the Golf Academy before they married; Vic Damone, George Abbott (Broadway's biggest producer); Billy Eckstine, Joey Bishop, and Danny Kaye. These were just a few of the celebrities that frequented the golf academy. The list goes on and on.

When I met Phil I knew nothing of his accomplishments, that he was known as "Mr. Broadway," or that he was considered the most distinguished and eligible bachelor in all Manhattan. I knew nothing about golf. Mother taught me to value a person for his goodness, not for his celebrity or for what he owned. What attracted me most to Phil was his love and devotion to our Catholic Faith. He was always crossing himself! We could not pass a Catholic Church without going inside, lighting a candle and praying a few prayers. I even noticed that whenever a pupil or someone else was leaving the academy, Phil made a small sign of the cross for every person behind their backs to receive blessings from God.

I have never stopped thanking or praising God for bringing Phil into my life because after we were married he brought with him all of the Catholic Traditions from Sicily. In the beginning our "chapel" was a few holy items on the top of a chest of drawers. A crucifix hanging in each room of wherever we lived, always reminded us that Jesus, the Man on the cross, was ever present.

Later Phil would build a real chapel in our home to house our collectibles and the holy items discarded by others. We eventually owned a life size statue of both, St. Therese the Little Flower and the Archangel Gabriel. A *mezuzah*, a small container that concealed a copy of the Ten Commandments, was nailed on the lintel of our front door. This is a Jewish Tradition, but following the Ten Commandments is an important part of our Catholic Faith, too. Phil's niece blessed us with a first class relic of St. Jude Thaddeus, Saint of the Impossible. The chapel became an invaluable place for our family to pray the rosary, for devotions and for passing on our Catholic values.

Shortly after we were married, I awoke one morning and recounted a strange dream. I described a little lady who was trying to give me a loaf of bread and asked me to get it blessed. Phil laughed. He said it sounded like his mother, Mama Rosa, whom I had never met because she died shortly before I met Phil. He said we would be celebrating Saint Joseph's Day with his family on Sunday, and that the bread always had to be blessed. He told me not to worry. His sister always made sure the bread was blessed. I took a loaf of bread to Saint Patrick's Cathedral and had a priest bless it just in case. When we arrived at his sister's home on Long Island, she was frantic. "*Mischina! Mischina!*" she cried. (Which means poor thing.) "Our feast is ruined! The priest had an emergency and our bread is not blessed!" I presented my blessed loaf which saved the day!

St. Joseph's day grew into a big celebration in our home with as many as two hundred friends and clergy joining our family. Two weeks before the feast day, I started preparing Italian specialties: bread baked in a form of St. Joseph's beard, St. Joseph's cream puffs filled with custard, struffoli, homemade stuffed sausage, and all kinds of pasta dishes, chicken cacciatore, veal parmesan, meatballs, and more were on the menu. Just like in Sicily, the feast began with a pageant. Three children dressed as Jesus, Mary, and Joseph knocked on the front door three times. Each time everyone shouted, "Go away! There is no room!" After the third time, the children were invited in and the one that was Jesus blessed the table. "Viva! Viva!" everyone shouted, as they began to fill their plates.

On August 1, every year Sicilians begin a novena leading up to the Feast of the Assumption on August 15. This is a time for fasting and offering special deeds up to Mary, for her intercession as she is known by one of her many titles, as the Queen of Heaven. This was also, a time to make sure everyone knew how to pray the rosary. During that time Mama Rosa used to sit on the stoop outside her apartment building in Brooklyn. It did not matter how old you were or what nationality or religion you had, Mama Rosa made sure everyone learned the prayers of the rosary.

On the eve of the Assumption, a simple feast of pizza and various traditional foods is served at midnight. Pots of water are set out because tradition has it that when Our Blessed Lady went up into Heaven, she blessed water everywhere. Throughout the Feast Day of the Assumption, part of the fun is blessing each other with water that is now considered Holy Water. It was a wonderful tradition we repeated with our family and brought the closeness of our faith and the love Jesus had for his mother to the forefront.

Our family celebrated a saint or Holy day, every day. The saints and the lives they lived became real to children and adults, alike. Especially when the stories were shared with enthusiasm, celebrated, and we watched spiritual transformations take place. On Saint Patrick's Day we always had green eggs and green bread for breakfast and Irish stew for dinner. A small pot of shamrock often graced our table.

As our children grew, the traditions we shared remained with them, and continued as adults. When traditions involve our Catholic Faith, they have the added bonus of fun and joy, coupled with learning the deeper truths of the teachings of Jesus Christ. Traditions helped my children fall in love with our Catholic faith. I was so blessed to be married to a man with a family whose ancestors passed on the Catholic faith through traditions that made faith real and tangible, so we could do the same with our children and friends.

UP TO THE MOUNTAINS

ife had already taken on a new meaning, when Paul Grossinger from the famed Grossinger's Resort located in Liberty, New York and in the Catskill Mountains asked Phil to be the golf director. The Galvano Golf Academy in the New York City would still be in operation. Golf in the Catskills could only be played six months at most because of the heavy snow and freezing temperatures in the other months. We planned to spend time in Florida during the winter months.

Phil was an important addition to the Grossinger's Resort. He was already famous as a golf professional, television star, author of four bestsellers, author of a daily newspaper column, and had helped start the Professional Golf Association of America. One thing Phil and the resort shared in common was their attraction of celebrities. Many celebrities visited the academy in the city and had become personal friends of Phil's. In the same way, many celebrities came to the resort not only to vacation but also to perform as entertainers in the nightclub. Many entertainers got their start performing at Grossinger's, such as Eddie Fisher, Jerry Lewis, and that's where Elizabeth Taylor met Eddie Fisher.

Grossinger's Resort also attracted famous athletes. Sonja Heine, an Olympic ice skating star, cut the ribbon for the opening of the ice skating rink. Irving Jaffe, a two-time Olympic speed skating star, was director of the skating rink. Florence Chadwick, known for swimming across the English Channel helped dedicate the swimming pool. "Boom-Boom" Mancini, Lightweight Champion of the World, and the United States Olympic gymnast and skiing teams were among many professional athletes to train at Grossinger's Resort.

The New York thruway made it easy to travel the one hundred miles back and forth from the city to the Catskills. One day Phil and I discovered a hundred acre farm for sale only two hilltops and four miles away from the resort. The two hundred year old farmhouse with a dugout basement, two huge barns and utility units were built with wooden pegs. The fields were in sections marked by three-foot tall rock walls that Indians had stacked up. Numerous apple trees dotted the fields. Fifteen acres of blueberries grew in a backfield. Pussy willow and white birch trees overshadowed two ponds. Wildflowers of all kinds bloomed in the fields and ditches. Deer, rabbits, a variety of birds and other wildlife shared the farm.

Phil and I knew from the onset the farm was meant for us. By this time we enjoyed our penthouse on the fourteenth-floor, overlooking Broadway and Times Square. Although we would miss seeing the huge balloon figures from the famous Macy's Thanksgiving Day Parade float past our terrace, we had no trouble giving it up for the farm. Phil would commute to the city when necessary. Since becoming a mother, life had taken on a new meaning for me. Living on the farm would be wonderful not only for Phil and me, but also, for the children. The only place the children could enjoy nature in New York City was Central Park, which consisted of constant noise of sirens and heavy traffic. There was no solitude anywhere except in church. My favorite childhood memories of feeling God's presence were when I lived in the country, at the "house in the sticks," and the memories never left me. For me the beauty and peace found in the quiet solitude in the countryside echoes God's words, "For God so loved the world that He gave his only Begotten

Son that we would not perish, but have everlasting life." The farm would be a little bit of Heaven on Earth!

In 1965 we made the move to the country in the Catskills. There was a lot of fixing-up to be done. Everything had to be painted. Hinges on doors had to be replaced. We were thankful the roof was in good condition; however some windows needed to be replaced as well. The well for our drinking water was cleaned out, and a door was added for the basement dugout to keep snow from covering the furnace. A gas tank was installed for cooking.

When we added a family room, part of the original wall of the house had to be exposed. We found the wall was covered with newspapers dating back to the 1700's! Next, the barns were painted and one was turned into a garage. Fences were repaired because an old Appaloosa horse and two ponies came with the farm. One pony was a miniature and perfect for the children to ride.

Our chapel in the city had been a dresser top, but now a small room off the kitchen was turned into a real chapel consisting of an altar with my collection of figurines of saints and a first class relic of Saint Jude Thaddeus. We added a wooden pew found in a junk shop. Phil made an iron altar rail at an iron works shop. This chapel would become very special to our family.

Father Mullin, a priest from St. Peter's Catholic Church in Liberty blessed our home and chapel. He was happy to have a stronger, Catholic connection to the Grossinger's Resort. The resort was strictly kosher where all of the major Jewish holidays were celebrated, but the guests were not all Jewish. When major conventions came to the hotel Father Mullin was often asked to celebrate Mass, in one of the conference rooms for the convenience of visiting Catholics. As for me, I would learn about our Catholic inheritance from the Jewish faith. I in turn, would share my Catholic faith in kind.

Phil and I must have looked like the couple from the television show, "Green Acres." News traveled fast on the countryside about our "showbiz" careers. Curious spectators often passed by the farm to catch a glimpse of the "city slickers." Phil was a city slicker and

I looked like one, but they would all find out that I was really a country girl!

An acre of land near the house was cleared and plowed over for a garden. As I was removing rocks and turning over the ground with a hoe, an old farmer came chugging by on his blue tractor. "Ain't nothing going to grow there! It's too wet!" I thanked him and smiled to myself. I had already anticipated spreading lime over the area to change the pH of the soil.

When I planted sixty tomato plants, the old toothless, farmer rode by again on his blue tractor to tell me that the plants were all going to die because a late frost had been predicted for the night. Later he saw me walking on my knees to each of the plants. He stopped his tractor and stared, as I am sure he wondered, *What in the world is she doing?*

Guess what? Everybody else on the countryside lost their plants. I did not lose one plant. One day the old farmer came by again. He asked me why I had been walking on my knees and why none of my plants had died. I told him I had been praying! *God hears every prayer.*

At harvest time, each plant produced a bushel of tomatoes. As a matter of fact, I won thirty-five blue ribbons at the Sullivan County Fair for my zucchini squash, cucumbers, corn, beans, peppers, eggplants and other vegetables grown in my garden. Besides prayer, part of the secret was that I had discovered four feet of dried up manure in the horse stalls in one of the barns!

Many evenings I could expect anywhere from ten to twenty guests and staff members from the resort to show up for dinner. I would invite the guests to go into the garden and pick the vegetables they would like me to cook. I would cook them fresh off the vines—and they loved it! In addition, I prepared fresh homemade bread and pies daily. Whenever I brought out the ice cream maker, everyone took turns churning the fresh blueberry mixture. We sat with our guests at a table under a big maple tree and enjoyed food, as well as fellowship. Often as twilight approached, deer sauntered by as the stars lit up the sky. Guests who had come up from the city often proclaimed what Phil and I already knew, "This farm is like heaven on earth!"

When Perry Como came to the resort to film a television commercial, he was so swamped by autograph seekers, he could find no peace. Perry asked to stay at our farm and asked us not to tell anyone. We were happy to accommodate him. That night I made *pasta fagiola* and a glorified hamburger, which our family still calls the "Perry Como Special".

One morning, five tractor-trailers and a dozen cars came plowing into the driveway. Phil had given Arnold Kaiser, CEO of the MPO Television Studios, permission to use our farm for a "Man Handler's" Campbell's Soup Commercial. Generators, electric cables and other equipment were unloaded. I was kicked out of the kitchen for the day while the television crew filmed actors eating soup, and then walking though the fields.

Occasionally, Phil asked me to play golf with some of his pupils and teach them course management. One such pupil was Johnny Carson from the *Tonight Show*. Another pupil was George Abbott, Broadway's biggest and best-known producer. George was eighty-four years old, at the time I played golf with him. He was amazing! One day he brought Maureen O'Sullivan, who played Jane in the movie, Tarzan with Johnny Weissmuller, out to the farm. Maureen was upset and excited at the same time. Mia Farrow, her daughter, had called that morning to tell her that she and Frank Sinatra had gotten married. George Abbot sometimes invited us to dinner at his hideaway in the woods near a lake in Monticello, only a few miles from our farm. His home consisted of four pagodas, Japanese Style. The largest pagoda contained a living room, kitchen and dining room. Dinner guests sat on cushions on the floor and at a low table. Each of the other pagodas contained a bedroom and a bath. All were connected by a wooden walkway. George Abbott rewrote one of his plays at 104 years old, he was amazing! He passed away at the age of 109 after living a very good and productive life.

George Abbott once offered me a movie role to play the life of Babe Zaharias, an Olympic track and field star, and golf professional.

I had to decline because I was pregnant with Philip and would not leave my family to go to Hollywood. When Bullets Durgom, Jackie Gleason's manager, asked me to star in *Horse Soldiers* with John Wayne, I had the same answer. I was then pregnant with Elizabeth. Hollywood and all its glamour could never be as exciting and fulfilling for me, as being a wife and mother with a very devoted husband. Phil and I trusted God and we knew He was guiding us. Our family was a gift from God and should always be cherished before all else. I have a very special place in my heart for all children, and believe every child is beautiful in his or her own way.

When Phil's family visited from the city, I hooked up our wagon to the back of our big red tractor and took the children for rides through the fields while they squealed and laughed. I loved giving the children a chance to experience the beauty of the country and the mountains, and wish all children had this opportunity.

It was not uncommon for me to occasionally see black and white milk-snakes, about eighteen inches long, following me through the yard. At first I was startled, but then a neighbor farmer explained that milk-snakes often were found in barns waiting to get milk from cows. We did not have a cow! Another day I nearly passed out when I walked into the kitchen. My daughter's friend's pony was drinking water from the kitchen sink! I quickly led the pony outdoors.

One time I arrived home to discover a deer across our large kitchen table. Phil had been hunting, and he knew I could butcher, and pack it for the freezer. Ugh! How did I tell my dear husband that while I was capable, it was a very large project! By the time I got through, the deer's hair and blood covered the kitchen! Out of courtesy for me, and at my gentle suggestion, Phil would take his future bounty to a butcher in town. Although I had my hunting license, I was never able to shoot anything, even if venison is delicious.

Holy Saturday, April 16, 1966, God blessed us with William Saint Galvano. Who needed an Easter basket when I was given a bassinet that held a newborn child, the most precious of all gifts? Ironically, that child born in Liberty would one day grow up to defend freedom and liberty as a Florida Legislator. Thirty of Phil's relatives arrived from Long Island to spend a week at the farm for a celebration; William's Baptism was performed by Father Mullin from St. Peter's Church, in our chapel.

March 4, 1968 Phil and I drove into the city for errands and an appointment with my obstetrician, as I was expecting our fourth child. Unexpectedly, the doctor immediately sent me to the Polyclinic Hospital. Poor Phil had to race a hundred miles back to Liberty to pick up Philip and Elizabeth who were in school. He was frantic and the hospital staff recounted how he called repeatedly, asking about my condition, until they finally could report I was fine, and had delivered the baby. However, hospital policy would not allow the staff to tell him if it was a boy or girl over the telephone. After dropping off our children with relatives, Phil finally arrived at the hospital. God had blessed us with Richard Douglas, our fourth child. When Dr. Vessel came to see me the next morning at the hospital, he told me my room was the very room which Rudolph Valentino had been in, when he died of peritonitis. I looked out the window to see where thousands of his fans lined up as far as I could see to mourn his passing. Interestingly, the doctor gave me excellent advice that day. He explained that children were being ruined with the trend of progressive education, which advocated letting a child make their own decisions with less parental authority. Dr. Vessel said to ignore the new ways and fads of upbringing; and instead use the tried and true method of plenty of love, plenty of discipline, and plenty of time. I agreed and truly that method worked well for our family.

Paul Grossinger and his wife, Bunny came to Richard's baptism which was also celebrated in our chapel, by Father Mullin. They celebrated St. Joseph's Day Feast with us and the Feast of the Assumption. They enjoyed our Catholic celebrations and traditional Italian foods. Phil and I sometimes celebrated Jewish

Holidays with them, and we enjoyed eating their kosher foods, as well.

During the week of August 15 through 18, in 1969, Max Yasgur, held the historic concert called "Woodstock," billed as a celebration of "peace and music." He sold tickets, but because more than 500,000 people showed up, and no one could control the crowd, the concert became a free-for-all during the height of what became known as the hippie generation! A few days before the concert, Phil and I took a drive to see what was happening. At the entrance to the farm we were shocked to see dozens of nude men, women and children swimming and playing in a muddy pond. During the concert, not enough food, water or toilets were available. The participants were so desperate they raked through gardens and orchards taking and eating whatever they could find. One cabbage farmer was not left with even one cabbage. Apple trees were stripped of their fruit, shops in town had to close because large numbers of hippies raked through the shops and took everything on the shelves. There was nothing the owners could do to stop them. Officials begged the community for help and while many of us sent food, there was nothing else we could do.

Drugs were the worse! One young man climbed a telephone pole at the concert and then dove off to his death. Many young people overdosed on drugs and were flown to the Grossinger's golf course by helicopter. Then they were taken to the area schools that were turned into make-shift hospitals. As soon as they were sober, they went right back to the concert to do more drugs. Traffic tied up the New York thruway and many slept on the medians of the highway. One man was run over by a car and it took a long time for the community to return to normal conditions. This tragedy was a sober reminder of the changing of times and how important it was for us to instill our faith and family values to our children.

DOWN TO THE SEASHORE
& THE COUNTRY CLUB

In 1969 we painstakingly made the decision to sell our farm and move to Bradenton, Florida, near Anna Maria Island. Since 1958, we enjoyed spending a few weeks every winter on Anna Maria, and Phil dreamed of one day having his own golf course. It was a giant leap, but with careful planning and some overcome obstacles, we purchased land on Cortez Road and Phil developed an Executive Golf Course. It was named the Santa Rosa Country Club after Mama Rosa, Phil's saintly mother. Mama Rosa passed away in 1954, and everyone in Phil's large Italian family held her in very high esteem. She had vigilantly passed on her Catholic Faith to everyone she met, especially her family.

In Bradenton our family could now participate in community affairs, especially church activities, unlike living in New York, where the weather prevented full participation with snowy and icy road conditions. At times it had even been difficult to drive to church. In Bradenton, we joined St. Joseph's Catholic Church, and often visited the church that reminded Phil of his childhood one in Brooklyn, the Sacred Heart Catholic Church. Both were wonderful, with holy and devoted pastors, and warm and friendly congregations.

In 1970, the Lord blessed us with Peter Bernard. In the years to come he became a perfectionist, whether it was his homework, golf practice, or just keeping his room neat. When Peter was a teenager, a visiting priest spent the night with us and he used Peter's room. He said that he picked up Peter's Bible lying on the night table to read. He thought he would find the pages stuck together, but instead he was impressed that the pages were thoroughly worn out! It is encouraging to know a child is on the right path.

In October of 1972 once again I felt new life within me; however the doctor's insistence that I end my pregnancy came as shock! This was the year Roe vs. Wade was passed. The doctor felt I was too old, at thirty-eight, and my "chemistry" was all wrong. I felt that a baby is a gift from God even if there are impending problems! The doctor was warning me I should prepare myself that I would have a Down's Syndrome, baby.

I was due the first of July, but by the end of July the baby still had not come. The doctor predicted the worse and yet I held on to the thought that no matter what, God would provide and was blessing our family. I was relieved when August arrived because our yearly, two-week novena to Our Lady would begin, and it would end on the fifteenth, the Feast of the Assumption. I knew in my heart the baby would be special and that the Blessed Mother was interceding for our family. Mary Frances arrived on August eleventh. She was a ten-month baby and perfect! The next night I sat on a green hassock in our family room cuddling the infant close to me as Phil and all the children sat around me, and we prayed the rosary to continue our novena in thanksgiving for this precious little miracle. Amazingly, we all noticed, Mary Frances, only a day old put her hands together and kept them there until we had finished our prayers! According to experts on child development, babies do not put their hands together until they are older. To our family this was a miracle and a sign to us from the Lord that He was with us.

There are many trials we survived as we raised our children, and it doesn't seem to matter if you have one or many. Being a good parent is a full time job because your thoughts are always on your children. For me, constantly talking with God and sticking close to your faith is the best advice I can give anyone raising a child. Not only will you bring your child closer to God, your child will bring you closer to God, as you learn to depend on Him. You may think that when a child is young with skinned up knees or a runny nose that is the time they most need prayers, but I recommend you never stop praying for your children—even, as they grow older. Their needs change, but not their need for prayers. Whenever I ask the Lord for guidance and help, I hear, in my heart the words, "on your knees." Sometimes I have wondered why my knees have not worn out!

Whenever I see parents with young children in church, I make it a point to tell them, "Bringing your children to church is the best thing you can do for them." I also advise them to sit near the front so the children will not be bored. Much of the time may be spent praying for them to behave, but it pays off—children are the future of the church.

Other trials struck our family as well. Peter almost died of pneumonia when he was ten. Philip almost died of appendicitis and then a car accident when he was a teenager. Elizabeth too almost died of pneumonia. Bill was shot with a BB that had to be cut from his tongue. When Richard was nine years old, he had a double hernia that three doctors considered dangerous enough to have an operation. The night before the surgery, Father Nugent prayed over Richard with our family asking for blessings on the doctors, nurses and whoever might be involved. When Richard was still in the operating room, the surgeon called the hospital room where Phil and I were waiting. He said that Richard had been cut open, but the hernia was gone! I responded that Father Nugent had prayed with him. The doctor said, "Prayers have already healed him!' The anesthesiologist, a confirmed atheist, still wearing his surgical clothes, came running into the hospital room. He wanted to know how to pray! Months later we learned that he was no longer an atheist! Perhaps God used the surgery for the soul of the doctor. Prayers healed the atheist, too!

Phil and I took our roles as parents seriously. The teachings of our Catholic faith came first. Everything else fell into place, as we gave our close knit family plenty of discipline, and plenty of love. All eight of us shared dinner together every night even when we had frequent guests. I did not believe the children should eat early or sit in the kitchen while the adults ate elsewhere. Each child took turns praying grace. Sometimes dinner would be at four o'clock, and sometimes it would be at ten o'clock, it depended on our scheduled activities. We expected shirts on for the boys, hair combed and clean hands and faces were a must. Whichever child needed the most help in improving his manners at the time, sat next to Phil who would give a reminder as needed. Each child shared whatever they had done that day, and today our children say one of the best things we ever did was to teach them manners and social graces. They are comfortable wherever they go.

Frequently, Phil invited guests to dinner, often they were famous such as Liberace, Willie Mosconi the World's Billiard Champion, Frankie Lane, Robert Merrill, the opera star, Billy Eckstine and Morey Amsterdam, who often joined our family entertainment which took place most nights after dinner. Phil always played the guitar and sang while I cleaned up. Elizabeth and Mary often sang and danced. Bill performed magic tricks and Phil often challenged the children to memorize or recite poems such as, "If" by Rudyard Kipling or speeches like "The Gettysburg Address." Phil, Bill, Richard, and Peter always entertained us in some way, as well.

On March 19, every year, guests joined us for a celebration of St. Joseph's Day a tradition that started with Phil's family. Sometimes as many as two hundred guests were in attendance. Priests and nuns from the church were always invited; in fact anyone who expressed a special love for the Holy Family was welcome.

The Santa Rosa Country Club and Driving Range was a success and always busy with golfers enjoying their game or trying to improve. Phil gave free use of the facilities to local school golf teams, including St. Joseph's School's Golf Team. The clubhouse was closed on Christmas or Easter and other holy days, but anyone could play free on the course, if they wanted to walk and carry their own bags on those days.

Once a friend who was dying told Phil, "Why, oh, why, did I spend so many Sunday mornings playing golf instead of going to church with my wife and children?" Phil thought that was a good question. Many happy golfers also have time for church.

Not surprisingly, all our children were among the top junior golfers in the state. Our trophy room was packed! The children were members of the Sarasota Junior Golf Association, and once when I went to pick the children up after a tournament at the Sunrise Golf Course in Sarasota, I was aghast! Richard looked like the Lochness Monster. He was covered with black muck after trying to retrieve his golf ball on the edge of a pond. When he stepped onto the soft mud, he sank up to his neck—it was quick sand! Everybody on the course ran to his rescue. It was quite an ordeal to pull him out.

When Peter was five-years old, he gave us a big scare! He was in a golf cart that slipped off a hill and slid into a pond eighteen feet deep. Peter jumped out of the cart just in time, but the golf course crew had to drag the pond for his clubs. He was playing in the USGA Junior Tournament at Disney World the next day and needed them—and despite this setback, Peter won the tournament!

The following is a true story about the time we lived in Bradenton. This story was published not only in the *Florida Catholic* but the *Catholic Digest*, as well.

PRAISE GOD! MY HOUSE IS ON FIRE!

Huge styrofoam snowflakes dangled from the fourteen-foot ceiling. Eight red stockings hung from the mantle. The Christmas tree glowed with dancing lights and tinsel. Everything was perfect until my attention was drawn to the nativity scene on the mantle.

I looked back at the pile of gifts under the tree and knew what was wrong.

"God," I prayed, "please do not let my children think Christmas is just a package under the tree." Little did I know what I was asking.

The next three weeks sped by...dance recitals, school plays, extra guests and parties, baking and more shopping. Then two days before Christmas, the children and I were returning from one last minute whirl at the mall. Three-year-old Mary and six-year-old Peter had wanted one more ride on the "Christmas Train" and to make sure Santa knew everything on their long lists.

Laughter and excitement filled our car. William, ten, and Richard, eight, scolded fifteen-year-old Philip and Elizabeth, fourteen, "There is so a Santa Clause!"

Suddenly sirens screamed from behind.

"God bless someone," we prayed in unison, as I pulled the car off the road to let two screaming and rushing fire engines race by. I pulled back onto the road. We found ourselves following the fire engines. When we turned the corner, we knew why. Our house was on fire!

Flames were shooting into the sky. Smoke poured from all angles. Firemen were everywhere...chopping doors with axes and spraying long streams of water over the growing flames.

"Mom!" screamed Elizabeth, pointing to a couple of firemen struggling across the lawn with someone. "It's Dad!"

My heart dropped as I pulled over and we all ran out of the car. I was beside Phil in moments.

"Thank God you and the children are safe," Phil muttered between coughs.

"Where's TiTi?" TiTi was William's little toy poodle. He was nowhere to be seen. Our eyes welled up with tears.

Just then, the roof collapsed with a thunderous roar. Phil, our six children and I were frozen in disbelief. Our home and everything in it was gone.

Do not let my children think Christmas is just a package under a tree, flashed across my mind. I started to cry because I knew God had heard my prayer, and now I knew that I needed to trust Him and look for His answer.

Father Nugent, our parish priest appeared at my side. "You must have faith," he emphasized, "God is with you."

Once the fire was out and the engines backed out of the driveway, we carefully stepped over piles of ashes and debris to enter the blackened shell of our once 5000 sq. ft. home. We stood in the roofless living room. The snowflakes, the tree, and all the presents were gone. Even our large family Bible was charred and smoking. I glanced at the mantle, now covered with ashes and a smoking rafter.

Carefully moving the rafter, I gently probed the ashes, and then smiled as I lifted out three sooty, weary, little figurines of Jesus, Mary and Joseph.

"Mom, it's like the first Christmas. Jesus, Mary and Joseph had no place to stay and neither do we," said Richard.

At that point I went to look at our chapel where some of our children had been baptized and where we had devotions. I was sure it was gone, for it was the room nearest to the gas heater that had blown up. Stepping over the debris, we picked our way to the chapel and feared the worse, but less than five feet away from the ruined heater, stood the closed door. I opened it. We gasped in disbelief. Not one single thing in the chapel had been harmed... no fire, smoke or water damage, and yet, the rest of the house was totaled.

That night we climbed into the bunk beds of our motor home that had been saved from near destruction. Young Philip broke the silence, "Dad, you know, there was a man named Job. He had everything like us, and when he lost it all, he didn't curse God, but kept on loving and trusting Him. God gave Job back more that he had ever had."

I wept again. First they were tears of joy of my young son's faith, then tears of loss for the material, the tree, the packages, the decorations and everything else.

Trust me, a silent voice within me whispered just before I fell asleep.

All the next day we sifted through ashes. Besides a picnic table and a few things from the kitchen, not much was left to take to take to a dilapidated house down the street that a friend had offered us. Friends, neighbors and strangers came to help. Many brought food, blankets, clothing and furniture. One lady even brought a small decorated tree.

"Are all these people Wisemen bearing gifts?" asked Peter.

"No, Peter, but they are sent by God bringing us real gifts of Christmas, gifts from the heart and gifts of love," I answered.

Besides the three tiny bedrooms, there was one other room which would be the kitchen, living room, the dining room, TV room and music room. The loaned house was run-down. Only one bathroom worked. Mattresses were brought in and bedspreads were tacked across the windows.

That night in "our stable," we were eating donated food with a couple of friends at our makeshift table. It was Christmas Eve. A whine came from the front door and William flung it open. TiTi jumped into his arms, licking his face.

"This is a Merry Christmas after all! We have each other and TiTi," he cried.

Suddenly, a tremendous explosion rocked that house. An unblocked gas line in a bathroom ignited, sending pieces of plumbing and fire throughout the house. I was literally blown out the front door and lay sprawled on the front lawn. Looking up, I heard screams and saw flames flashing through a window. The three youngest boys were trapped by fire in a back room. TiTi was on fire!

Precisely at that moment, a small white car slammed to a stop in front of the house. A man and a woman both dressed in white dashed out. Then the man helped me to my feet, rushed into the house and rescued the boys and TiTi. He called the fire, gas and police departments. When they arrived he directed them, blocking off three streets leading to the house in case of floating gas pockets.

All the while I was frantic. Mary was missing! The woman in white suddenly blocked my path. Looking me straight in the eyes and placing a firm hand on my shoulder, she said. "Don't worry. He is a professional."

The only other thing I heard the woman say was, "We must hurry. We have so much to do," as she wrung her hands.

Professional what? I wondered later after finding Mary and Elizabeth at a neighbor's house. Even today questions linger. How did the man and woman arrive at the exact moment of the explosion? How did the man make calls on an out of order phone? Why were they both wearing white, and how did they disappear so suddenly?

Father Nugent appeared at my side and once again encouraged me, "Don't be afraid! Angels are watching over you! I want you at Mass in the morning," he emphasized.

Christmas morning we squeezed into the front row of the crowded Sacred Heart Church. Our clothes were dirty, smoky, and shabby. They were the ones we had worn for three days. My hair was in tangles, we were a mess.

When Father Nugent placed the Holy Eucharist on my tongue, a silent voice within me whispered, "The Holy Eucharist is my gift to you. This is what Christmas is all about...Jesus."

Weeks went by, then months. What was left of our old house was cleared away and a new one started. We continued to live in the borrowed house. Finally, in August, during our annual novena, we moved into our new home. Father Cronin, an elderly Irish priest ninety years old who looked like a leprechaun saw me in the super market. "My dear, I have just returned from Ireland. I have a gift for you. May I bless your house tomorrow afternoon?" He asked.

Pleasantly surprised, I answered "Why yes. Thank you."

By the time Father Cronin had finished blessing our home, everything was dripping with holy water...the cars, the trees, and bushes. It even ran down our noses. Father left us a framed house blessing, which read:

"O Lord God Almighty, bless this house. In it may there be health, chastity, victory over sin, strength, humility, goodness of heart and gentleness, full observance of Your law and gratefulness to God, the Father, the Son and the Holy Spirit. And may this blessing remain upon this house and upon those who live here, now and forever and ever. Graciously send Your Holy Angel from Heaven to watch over, to cherish, to protect, to abide with, and to defend all who dwell in this house."

That night I sat reading in the living room. Everyone else was asleep. Suddenly, a strange cry echoed through the house. I sprang from my chair to grab one of my sons who was running towards me.

His eyes were wide on his white face. "I saw it!" He exclaimed.

"Saw what?" I asked as the rest of the family came out to see what was wrong.

"The angel! I got up in the dark, went to the bathroom and when I came back to my bed, someone with dark curly hair, blue eyes and a white robe was standing by my bed. I could see the legs of my desk chair through the bottom of his robe!"

"Don't be afraid," I answered. "Father Cronin blessed our home." I picked up the framed House Blessing and began to read it aloud. "Whether you saw anyone or not it doesn't matter...because if you did, it has to be the angel Father Cronin invited into our home."

The children returned to bed. I sat quietly alone pondering the events of the last ten months. If I had been told our home would be destroyed, I would have pleaded with God not to let it happen. But it did happen. And truthfully despite the tragedy, it was a wonderful Christmas.

A GENTLE TOUCH OF HIS MIGHTY HAND

n 1980 our family moved to Sebring, Florida which was seventy miles away from Bradenton located in the middle of the state. A few years later, Phil would sell his Golf Course, in Bradenton. He thought Sebring, a golfing community, offered many opportunities for our entire family. Philip, Richard, and Peter would all turn professional and join the Professional Golfers Association (PGA). Elizabeth and Mary would join the Ladies Professional Golf Association (LPGA). They all had dual professions. Although Bill was good enough to be a professional golfer, he chose to concentrate on being an attorney. My golf had improved enough to be a club champion and to win the Ladies Central Florida Championship sponsored by a local bank.

Phil added a room to our home to include a golf cage where he would continue to give golf lessons to pupils coming to him from many parts of the country. Then, he could take them right out onto the golf course across the street for further instructions. Some pupils slept over, ate with us and joined our family entertainment at night.

Our home, on the edge of Little Lake Jackson was hidden from the street by a long driveway and bushes. All kinds of wildlife, squirrels, alligators, possums, raccoons, armadillos, snakes and birds of all kinds enjoyed living there, too. Every morning before anyone else was up, I sat on the back patio with my cup of coffee for my devotions: Bible reading, praying the rosary and saying good morning to Jesus. A bald eagle often looked down from the tree above. Sparrows and blue jays sometimes pecked at the crumbs of my toast that was sitting on a plate next to me.

Our chapel was accessible by the door off of the garage. We were amazed one day when a white dove flew into the garage, through the open kitchen door, around the dining room table and then back to the chapel. He flew up and perched on the arch over the chapel. For the next three months he slept there. In the mornings he flew away, but each evening he was back. One day he just did not come back. The dove was a constant reminder of the Holy Spirit that appeared when Jesus was baptized by John the Baptist.

Once when one of our children was away and confronting a major problem, I could not sleep. I had stayed up most of the night walking back and forth praying my rosary. I walked out on the patio. Something hit me on the head. I picked it up. It was a six-inch cross! Granted a squirrel in the tree from above had crafted it, but it was enough to remind me to trust Him. Miraculously all worked out well for my child.

Life continued on and Phil was in the process of writing another book. He had his weekly column for a syndicated newspaper, and I was his typist. I took classes and graduated from the Writer's Digest School and the Advanced Writer's Digest School. My instructor, Woodeene Koenig-Bricker, a devout Catholic and Editor of *Catholic Parent Magazine*, a Sunday Visitor Publication, asked me to write for the magazine. I wrote articles for the magazine for fifteen years. Woodeene and I became good friends.

Greg Erlandson, editor and publisher of *Our Sunday Visitor*, asked Woodeene to have me write this article about my special ordeal, after he had read about it in the *New York Times*. It appeared in the *Catholic Parent Magazine* July/August 1999.

ZAPPED BY THE SPIRIT

As soon as I heard the cracking sound, I knew my hip was broken. That July morning, I had risen before the rest of the family, taken my Bible, my rosary and a cup of coffee and gone out to the back patio, which faced the lake at the edge of our property. As I stood in wonder, the huge ball of fire, the sun, sent flames of red rays dancing across the still water. Mesmerized by the sight, I left our patio, walked through the yard and jumped over the seawall to a sandy beach area to be nearer the awesome scene.

After a few minutes on the beach, I attempted to jump back up onto the 3-foot seawall protecting our yard from the wilderness beyond. It was then I lost my footing and fell.

As sharp pains shot through my right hip and leg, I began to feel a tickling sensation and then biting stings. I had fallen directly on an anthill! I tried to brush off the stinging creatures, but they clamored over me, biting and stinging until tears came to my eyes.

But that wasn't the worst. I knew that venomous snakes and alligators inhabited the small lake just down the sandy beach. Just the other morning, I had seen a nearly 10-foot gator slide silently into the water not far from where I now lay.

Despite the fact I knew no one could hear me, I began to shout for help. But it was no use. Even if they could have heard me, no one was awake. I grabbed at clumps of grass and tried to pull myself away from the ants, but all I succeeded in doing was stirring them up more. The pain in my hip grew worse. I lay on my back and stared into the sky.

Suddenly, there was a loud grunt. I looked toward some tall, thick weeds at the water's edge. The weeds swayed back and forth as something moved through them. Another grunt rumbled through the brush, and I knew an alligator was nearby.

Frantically, I grabbed at the clumps of grass and tried again to pull myself away from the approaching danger. The ants kept biting. The pain in my hip grew worse.

"Please, God, help me!" I screamed. I looked back at the weeds. They no longer moved, but I knew that somewhere just out of sight I was being watched...and stalked.

I screamed for help again and again.

The sun rose higher, and I knew that my family would be rousing soon. I also knew from the occasional sway of the reeds that the alligator continued to bide his time just beyond my sight.

The, sun now golden, was quickly getting higher. A mocking bird curiously swooped over me and settled on a nearby cattail. He sang. I, too, raised my voice to God and cried out, "I don't care what happens. I'll never stop loving You!" and began shouting for help again. Just then my daughter, Mary burst from the house. She had been sleeping when I came on the patio and miraculously she had heard my plea for help from her bathroom window.

She helped me sit up and brushed some of the ants away. With her help I painfully hopped on my left leg back toward the house. I had been lying on the beach for more than two hours.

Later that morning, at the hospital, the doctor confirmed I had broken my right hip where the femur joined it. Before the doctor could operate on me, he had to put my leg in traction to get it into the right position. For three days, I laid in a hospital bed with a heavy weight pulling on my leg.

The throbbing pain turned into agony. When I could bear it no longer, I called out to God. "Why me?"

"Why not you?" came the answer. Suddenly the throbs of pain became the rhythm of a hammer pounding nails into the cross. I thought of Jesus, and the pain became more bearable.

On the morning of my operation a priest anointed me with oil. I saw the prayerful and concerned expressions on the faces of my husband, Phil, and daughter, Mary. We all knew there was a chance I might not walk again.

Mary removed the rosary from my hand. As a nurse rolled me away on a stretcher to the operating room, I silently prayed the words I had spoken on the beach, "I don't care what happens, I'll never stop loving you!"

When the operation was over, the doctor had attached two ten-inch steel bars to my femur and hip. For the first six months, I used a walker to get around and then a cane. Finally, eleven months after the accident, I no longer used the cane, but I walked with a pronounced limp. Whenever I stood up to walk, I grimaced, and said, "Now," as I tried to move my leg. It often dangled like a heavy sandbag at my side, but the doctors assured me that I was lucky to be able to move at all.

On Saturday June 11, nearly a year after the accident, Phil and I were visiting two sons who lived in Fort Myers, Florida. I had been to confession and the 3:30 vigil Mass at St. Francis Xavier Catholic Church. At approximately 5 p.m., Phil and I were in the kitchen of our sons' home. Phil was sitting at a table in the corner of the room about six feet away from me. I was standing in front of the dishwasher near the sink, cutting fresh broccoli. No appliances were on.

The window over the sink was slightly opened, and sunshine came through the partially closed blinds. Although we lived in the storm capital of the country, none of us knew there was a storm in the area. I continued to cut the broccoli and chat with Phil when I was literally rocked off my feet by a tremendous clap of thunder. The knife in my hand flew one way, the broccoli flew another way. I was tossed about the kitchen and then slumped over the counter. I felt as if thousands of needles had entered the toes and foot of my right leg. The sensation traveled up my leg to the 10-inch bars that had been inserted during my operation. After a number of jerks in my upper leg, the needle sensation went away. My right foot and leg were now numb.

I clung to the edge of the sink and murmured, "I've been hit by lightning." I then collapsed.

Phil dragged me to the couch. He began patting my face. Slowly, as I was regaining consciousness, I looked out over the backyard, through the large glass doors of the living room, the sun was still shining, and the end of the rainbow had touched down in the yard.

Gold particles were swirling around the rainbow. There was no sign of a storm. I began to wonder if I were, in fact dying.

Phil began rubbing my foot and leg. Gradually the numbness went away and the feeling returned to my leg and foot. When I realized I was still alive, I stood up and took a step. To my amazement, my leg no longer dragged. As Phil watched, I walked, then danced about the house.

No trace of a limp remained. My leg had been energized. I had been healed.

A doctor in Fort Myers who examined me was amazed, but said that since shock treatments are often used to restore muscles and nerves, I miraculously got what I needed to restore function to my leg by the lightning bolt. Two doctors put on my medical charts, "healed by lightning." He also believed I had died for a few seconds.

Since being hit by lightning, I am appreciative of each moment of every day. I thank God for everything. I feel his Presence ever with me. I want nothing more than to love and serve Him with my whole heart. Every day, I pray the prayer I said on the beach, "I don't care what happens. I'll never stop loving You!" However, when I know a thunder storm is approaching or there is any lightning in the area, I will not venture outdoors, and I use safety measures indoors.

The morning after being hit by lightning, Phil and I again went to Mass. When we told our parish priest what had happened, he said, "Zapped by the Spirit!"

That is the only explanation I have, too, "Zapped by the Spirit" and a "Gentle Touch of His Mighty Hand."

Discovery, Pax TV, Unexplained Mysteries, and Fugi Television from Japan produced special shows highlighting my story as an unexplained phenomenon. *Good Housekeeping Magazine* and the *New York Times* also ran the story.

SAFELY HOME

I n the fall of 1991, Phil received a life-changing and devastating call from his doctor. Phil had cancer and was only expected to live three to six months. However, only God knows the day and time He chooses to call us home, and Phil outlived the dire predictions, living another three-and-a-half years. While we still lived in Sebring, we remained very close to our now adult children, spending every weekend visiting those who either lived in the Fort Myers or in the Bradenton area.

Phil began a process of saying good-bye, by getting in touch with special people in his life. His sister and all the relatives who lived in the Ft. Lauderdale area, begged me to drive him down for a family gathering. At first Phil was reluctant because he believed many of his younger relatives had forgotten him, however his sister, Faye, and niece Joyce thought otherwise.

We found about forty relatives along with Father William Collins, upon our arrival. The day was spent eating a scrumptious Italian feast, sharing stories, praying the rosary and special prayers with intercession requests to St. Joseph and St. Therese, the Little Flower, who were among Phil's favorites. As we pulled out of the driveway to head back home, Phil told me how touched he was by all the love and affection his family showed him. The day was a joyful remembrance and anticipation of the days to come.

Life continued onward and when my friend Joyce, who owned and operated a Catholic Religious Store in Ft. Lauderdale, answered my question, "What is your bestselling object?" Her answer surprised me when she said anything to do with angels. She then commissioned me to make angels for her store. This was absurd, as I never considered myself a craft person, in the least! A couple of weeks later Joyce begged me again to make angels for her store.

Since I was spending every moment I could with Phil and was homebound, I had extra time. One morning I cut up two of my old evening dresses to make dresses for little angels I was creating with woodenheads, pipe stems and gold wings cut from a cardboard box. I autographed "Elizabeth" on each one and attached a card that read, "This angel has been made with prayer for the owner to have peace, love, and joy." I mailed off forty-eight little angels, and thought, *Mission accomplished!*

At least I *thought* the mission had been accomplished, until Joyce called to tell me four more stores in Ft. Lauderdale wanted my angels! My business, the "Joyful Angels" had been born. Within four months the angels were in four countries and twenty-seven states, only something the Lord could arrange, especially from a person with no craft experience! I was making angels for people requesting them to be made out of their wedding dresses, and even clothing of deceased children. A friend who was involved in an AIDS' mission in New Jersey gave them to dying patients. An antique dealer gave me bisque heads to make angels that he sold at a very high price. Orders for angels came from golf shops, boutiques, Christmas Shops, Mote Marine and friends. Even the *Ritz Carlton* ordered them for shops in three hotels. My prayer card was attached to each one as a reminder for those who received them to have peace, love and joy.

Phil was getting weaker, when he expressed a desire to see our son, Phil, and he asked if I would drive him to Wisconsin Dells, where our son operated another Galvano Golf Academy. I was glad Mary came with us in case I needed help. While we were there I was asked to make Indian angels. On the drive back to Florida, Phil surprised me by asking to stop in Birmingham, Alabama to visit the Eternal Word Television Network (EWTN). I gave Mother Angelica an eight-inch angel dressed in yellow, her favorite color. Mother Angelica graciously accepted it. She kept that angel on her coffee table during her television show for many months.

The lady that ran the EWTN gift shop placed an order for angels from me. While we were talking, another lady came into the shop and bought a prayer card. Without saying a word, she dropped it into my purse and left. The two of us were perplexed! Neither one of us knew that lady, when I picked the card out of my purse I found it had a picture of Kateri Tekakwitha, a little Indian girl soon to be canonized as a saint. I knew I had to make Indian angels! I felt compelled to pray to Kateri Tekakwitha for intercession, since I had no idea how to create them. It wasn't long before I was shipping Indian angels to Wisconsin!

I prayed the angel ministry was a reminder to pray for our Catholic clergy, especially for our pope, cardinals, bishops, priests, nuns or anyone else passing on the faith. So, I sent an angel dressed in white satin and gold trimmings with my prayer card to Pope John Paul II. I did not anticipate a response. I was delightfully surprised when the pope sent me a letter and an Apostolic Blessing, especially now that he is Saint John Paul II!

There was one more trip we needed to make to visit Elizabeth and her husband, Jeff, who lived near Orlando. They were involved in a youth ministry there and through the years they have been responsible for helping change the lives of many teenagers. Elizabeth was known for her cooking, and Jeff went all out to please us with "Benedictine hospitality."

As Phil became more ill, we stayed with Richard and Peter in their home in Ft. Myers, near Phil's doctor. All of the children wanted to spend as much time as they could with him. Bill and his wife, June had to remain in Bradenton, since she was about to give birth to our first grandchild.

It was Holy Week and I was sitting at Phil's bedside praying the Stations of the cross out loud for him to hear, when I looked at him. He was lying in a hospital bed that Hope Hospice had brought into the home. I gasped! "Oh, God, You have already taken Phil!"

For a brief moment I did not see Phil at all, in my mind I saw only Jesus! Phil's hair was longer than usual, he had a loin-cloth, his feet were crossed and with his left hand he stroked his head, as though there was a crown of thorns. What a revelation! Since our first day of Holy Matrimony, we always considered ourselves as one. I now understood that while neither Phil nor I were perfect, what kept us so in love with each other was Jesus living within us. We were bound together as one by our love for Jesus!

At four a.m., Wednesday morning I awoke from a dream and went into the kitchen. In my dream I was standing before the brilliant golden gates of Heaven. The gates slowly opened. I then saw the backs of Phil, an angel without wings, and Jesus, as Christ the King, wearing a white robe and a crown. They stood in front of a clear body of water flowing from two throne chairs on a hill. A lady cloaked in brown came beside me. When I asked her why she was there, she answered she had been doing this since 1897. Then her cloak opened and her dress was covered with pink roses. I knew she had to be St. Therese the Little Flower. Then I woke up.

I picked up my Bible and began to read the last chapter of Revelations. I read that the river of life-giving water, clear as crystal, issued from the throne of God and of the Lamb. The same chapter says, "Remember, I am coming soon. Happy the man who heeds the prophetic message of this book." I held these words close to my heart.

Later I found out that one of St. Therese's promises was to escort souls to Heaven! Father Anglim told me this dream was not imagination, but revelation because I had received a date. Bill called from the hospital in Bradenton. We put the phone to Phil's ear. Tears filled his eyes as he smiled. He heard Michael's firstborn cry.

Near midnight Richard called my attention to Phil's head. It was tilting. I cradled his face in my hands, as I attempted to move his head. As I did so, Richard said, "Dad just took his last breath." Later I would find out that one of the promises of the devotion for the Feast of the Assumption was that one would die in the hands of a loved one! Phil had been born on All Saints Day and had died on Holy Thursday. Earlier Father Anglim visited Phil. He said Phil would not die on Good Friday. That day would be reserved for Jesus.

The funeral had to wait until the Monday after Easter. Bill drove Julie and the infant from the hospital to the wake at the funeral home. Bill placed Michael in my arms. My tears fell, as I walked up to the casket, holding this precious gift. I knew Phil had to be smiling. I wondered if their souls had met, as one was leaving this earth, and the other was arriving.

Father Anglim graciously suggested and the parents agreed to baptize Michael on Easter Sunday, before the funeral. This special arrangement was a wonderful blessing, since we did not know when all of our family could be together again.

Mary, as a child, had learned to sing with Phil when he played his guitar in the evenings. She was a cantor at St. Francis Xavier Catholic Church. Mary had never sung the Ave Maria and the liturgy more beautifully than she did that day for her father. I don't know how she kept so composed. Phil, Bill, Richard, and Peter all gave touching eulogies. Elizabeth was a great comfort to all of us with the warmth of her God given spirit through her tender words to each of us. We were tearful, and in our aching hearts we knew God was with us, and we knew Phil wanted us to be strong and to carry on. Phil had been the best loving, devoted husband and father. When the children still lived at home, he could be found in the middle of the night going from room-to-room and praying for each of our sleeping children. We knew he would continue to pray for us, as he had always done.

Although there would be a void in our lives, we rejoiced and knew in our hearts that Phil would always be with us, and he had made it, safely home.

TOTALLY HIS

The weekend was over and I was back in Sebring. The garage opened as the door slid up. I gave a scream, kicked a chair and threw a pillow, and then I began to pack boxes, as I would do for the rest of the week, until I went back to Fort Myers to spend the weekend with my children. This was the ritual I would perform for several months before I could move to Fort Myers.

There was no point for me to continue to live in Sebring. I needed to be close to my family. Mary and I planned to buy a small house in Fort Myers. She was a cantor at St. Francis Xavier Catholic Church and I loved everything about that church. I looked forward to being involved and for the first time I stood alone in our home as a widow, and I asked God, "What am I to do?" In my heart I knew I was now totally His and I told Him so.

As much as my children wanted to help me, it was hard for them to get away from their jobs. My sole companion was a magnificent black cat who appeared one day, as a scrawny little thing, when I was working in the flower garden. I tried to find his owner with no luck. The animal shelter said they would have to put him to sleep. I decided to keep him. One of my sons gave him the name, Napoleon, because as he grew, he looked so regal strutting about the yard. Now, Napoleon never left my side, as I packed. If I were packing a box, he was in it. If I were typing, he sat on the desk. Even when I stepped on the scale, he stepped on it, too! Every chance he had, he sat in my lap licking my arm. Napoleon gave me great comfort. I felt God sent him to me for company. God knows our every need.

An insurance agent was coming one day to inspect a small sinkhole that had developed near a wall next to the swimming pool. A plant had grown up that blocked the view of the hole. Before the agent arrived, I took a hoe out to the spot and with one big swing chopped the plant away. The plant flew up into the air, and so did a rattlesnake! The snake had been wrapped around the bottom of the plant. The snake about two feet long, brushed my shoulder, as it fell to the ground. Then it landed about eighteen inches from my feet. I was trapped! I was standing in a corner of the wall. The snake's tail rattled loudly, as his fangs threatened me. I stared into the snake's eyes and prayed, "Please do not let me die here and alone." I stayed perfectly still, it was an eternity or so it seemed, but in reality only twenty or thirty minutes went by, the snake stopped rattling his tail and slithered away. I ran screaming through the yard, as I released my tension!

Mary and I soon moved into a little house near my sons' home. Besides being a cantor at church, she was employed as a LPGA golf professional. I became involved volunteering wherever needed at St Francis Xavier Catholic Church. I also became a dedicated Hospice Volunteer and sat with dying patients. Many patients are afraid to die alone, and I could gently comfort them, by explaining there is nothing to fear. With those who I knew were Catholic, we prayed the rosary together, and I explained, "Jesus is waiting with open arms."

I especially liked attending services with the Hospice Honor Guard Team for World War II, Korean, Vietnam and other veterans. The veterans are honored for having protected our country, our Religious Freedom and assured that their sacrifice had not been lived in vain.

At Father Anglim's request, I enrolled in the newly formed Diocesan Rice School of Barry University to study theology and ministry. I graduated in 1998. Besides being a lector, Eucharistic Minister, and First Communion teacher, I totally embraced the Council of Catholic Women (CCW) and have served for over twenty years in many different capacities. I consider the CCW to be the finest women's organization in the world. Besides the marvelous works the women do, the women are a spiritual sisterhood. I know I could go anywhere in the world and if there is a CCW, I can call on them if I need help.

The Council of Catholic Women was formed by the United States Bishops, in 1920 during World War I when many men were off fighting in the war and the Church needed helpers. When the war was over the Bishops saw the power of Catholic Women, and started the National Council of Catholic Women. This is a worldwide organization and sisterhood dedicated in spirituality, leadership and service and under the guidance of our Bishops. Our Mother of Good Counsel is our patron, as we strive to be the voice of Catholic Women.

In 1998 the Council of Catholic Women, at Father Anglim's request, put in a prayer garden, an entire acre, at the church. That year the NCCW at the national convention awarded our local council the one and only national prize of a thousand dollar scholarship to be given to a college student who was studying the environment. I gave spiritual garden tours to various groups and ran a children's garden club for twelve years. Bishop Nevins of our Diocese visited often. He was always interested in the names of the flowers because it was believed that the flowers had once been named after the Blessed Mother. After the Reformation, the names were changed, but the former names have slowly been returning. When I till the soil I feel like I am tilling my soul.

When my mother was dying, I went to Greenville, South Carolina. She shocked me when she confided that she had always wanted to become Catholic! Grandmother would have disowned her! My mother's father had passed away when she was an infant, and I remember stories about how they lived in the Widow's Home in Augusta, Georgia, but for the first time I learned it had been run by

Catholic Nuns! Mother said she had never forgotten many things the nuns taught her or the walks in the woods to pick flowers. Mother had taught me many of their ways and vicariously lived her desires to become Catholic through me. My youngest sister also married a Catholic. June did not experience the prejudice I had experienced.

Once when Phil and I drove to Florida, we stopped to visit Grandmother in Atlanta. It was bittersweet. She bent over me sitting on a chair in her home, pointed a finger to my face and said, "I can forgive you for anything that you might have done in your life, but not for becoming Catholic!" Those were her last words to me. That was over fifty years ago. I have her picture on my wall, pray for her often and love her anyway. Somehow I believe she now understands my love for our Church. I like to believe Grandmother has changed her mind and loves it, too! All of her ancestors were from Ireland. Sister Agnes, a nun living in Knock, Ireland once told me, "If anyone digs deep enough, he will find the bones of his Catholic ancestors!"

Mother said she had greatly admired my husband Phil as well as June's husband, Tony, for practicing the Catholic Faith, sending their children to Catholic Schools and being everything a Christian father and husband should be. Mother said by our example we had convinced her, that she still wanted to be baptized a Catholic. Mother asked me to have a priest come to the hospital. One came and she was baptized a Catholic. Mother said she could now die happy!

On the drive back to Florida, another one of my heartfelt desires was fulfilled. Mary and I stopped to visit the Sacred Heart Church where I had been converted. I had not been back since the day of my conversion. St. Joseph's Infirmary had moved to the outskirts of Atlanta, but the church was still there. The life size crucifix still hung over the altar and myriads of colors still danced throughout the church as sunlight shone through the magnificent rose window from the back. A Mass was beginning. As I took communion, I nearly froze. I looked up at Jesus on the cross. My heart was bursting with joy! I was receiving Him in the exact spot He had called me to himself during my conversion, yes, I was totally His and I always will be!

In 1997 Mary and I went on a pilgrimage to Poland and attended the Eucharistic Congress. We would never be the same. First, was the visit to Auschwitz, the concentration camp. The day was dismal with a slight drizzle, a perfect atmosphere for the atrocities that had taken place. I still carried the pain and sorrow I had as a child during World War II when I often had cried myself to sleep upon hearing the events of the war. Outside the window of Saint Maximillian Kolbe's cell, where he suffered so much for the Faith, there was a short wall where prisoners were often executed. I knelt at the wall and let my tears fall. As I prayed for all the souls that had lost their lives there, suddenly joy replaced the pain that I carried for many years. This was a healing moment for me. I now understood they had suffered for the love of God and they will live with Him forever.

Another highlight, on a happier note, was that Mary sang the liturgies for at all of our Masses in Poland, including before the American Delegation in the crowded Cathedral of Krakow. There was a sea of clergy, hundreds of priests, cardinals, bishops and other religious in attendance. Pope John Paul II, now a saint, was there in an adjoining room!

Mary sang for the Sisters of Divine Mercy before the portrait of the Divine Mercy at Saint Faustina's Chapel, at the Jasna Gora Monastery, a national shrine for the Black Madonna and at Prague for the Chapel of the Infant of Prague.

Two years later Mary and I went on a pilgrimage with Father Anglim to the Holy Lands. Father Peter Vasko, our Franciscan Guide told us, as we rode the bus up the hill from the airport to Jerusalem that if we were thinking we had planned this trip, we were wrong. He said that God had planned this pilgrimage long ago and at this particular time. He said we had been brought there for our hearts to be touched, healed and for direction from God. He said that for now, our visits to the shrines might seem short, but that our longest visits would be in our memories. As our bus climbed the steep incline towards Jerusalem that could be seen by its lights on the hilltop, Mary sang "The Holy City, Jerusalem!" Once again, on this pilgrimage, Mary was invited to sing the liturgies for all our Masses.

We stayed in a hotel in Galilee. Our room was on the fourth floor and had a balcony overlooking the Sea of Galilee. In the middle of the night, I woke up, so I woke Mary up, as well.

"It's four a.m.!" she complained.

"Mary, let's look for fishermen!" I begged.

Reluctantly, she walked out on the balcony with me. All of a sudden shooting stars of all colors and sizes filled the sky. The stars were red, yellow, green, white, and every other color. We ducked as some seemed to be heading for our very room. The next morning we told the rest of our group what we witnessed. They just laughed and said, "Oh, you are always seeing things!"

The next morning they took back those words. The USA Newspaper that arrived a day late in the Holy Lands carried the story of the phenomenon we witnessed. The article said that every thirty-three years there is a special meteor shower. The last place to have seen this was over Texas. This time it had been over the Holy Lands. Ten thousand shooting stars of all colors and sizes had filled the sky that night! To this day I know the Lord allowed me to wake up because He wanted me to enjoy the glory of His creation. Perhaps He sent a guardian angel to wake me up, but either way I enjoyed this, especially with my daughter.

Father Peter was right. There is not a day that goes by that I do not have longer visits to the shrines of the Holy Lands. Being re-baptized in the Jordon River where John the Baptist had baptized Jesus warmed every fiber of my body, even though the temperature of the water was cold.

As I stood in the hot sun overlooking the red sand of the Qumran and the black holes of the caves where the Dead Sea Scrolls had been found, I thought: *No wonder John the Baptist and the Desert*

Fathers, like St. Jerome, spent so much time here—the peace was amazing and there was now nothing here, but God.

Standing on the shore of the Dead Sea, I trembled. The Dead Sea is the lowest point on earth. It was once vibrant with life—now nothing lives in the water that is so laden with salt that nothing alive can survive. Sodom and Gomorrah, thriving cities had been located on the shore. Because of disobedience to God they were destroyed, and the sea became dead.

Experiencing the Holy Land and touching the walls of the buildings that Jesus touched, holding the sand he had walked upon, smelling flowers he had smelled, and hearing the birds call, are but a few of my memories. To date nothing compares with picking an olive leaf from the Garden of Gethsemane—and carrying a cross on the Via Dolorosa, either. Yet these memories live on and I return to them over and over, as Father Peter Vasko had said I would.

On August 9, 2004 all of Florida was warned and put on high alert as Hurricane Charlie barreled down, toward the coast of Florida. Charlie, a Category Three, storm was coming with a fury! Charlie packed winds up to 150 miles an hour as it left the Caribbean Sea and began traveling up the west coast of Florida. People scurried everywhere getting supplies, boarding up windows, getting food, flashlights, and batteries, as they secured their homes and businesses. Friday the thirteenth as the storm was heading up the west coast of Florida and directly for Fort Myers, Charlie veered a little to the north towards Punta Gorda twenty miles away, saving our area from the full force of the winds. However, the winds caused catastrophic damage throughout the state.

Mary, Princess, her toy poodle, and I retreated to a back bedroom closet in our home. We took pillows, flashlights, a short wave radio, bottles of water and sandwiches. While we sat in the dark closet, the house shook, as loud, bumping sounds hit the roof and sides of the house. Huge crashes banged against all sides. Thunder with heavy rain seemed to be pounding everywhere. We listened to an alert on our radio and prayed. The storm was now on top of our neighborhood! Five and a half hours later we cautiously emerged from our shelter. Only the walls and floor of our home remained intact. Seven huge pine trees had fallen in the yard. One pine tree with a huge possum sitting on it had fallen into the kitchen!

I sat down on a chair in the kitchen. As the rain came down like a waterfall hitting the stove, I knew I had to try to get to Teco Arena, a planned shelter. I knew I would be needed, as I had been trained as a Red Cross Volunteer. Over six thousand refugees filled the sports arena. I helped register hundreds of refugees, many in total shock. With other Red Cross workers, we fed people, and gave them roll-a-way beds and ministered to them in many ways.

Mary and I too were refugees, living mostly out of our cars in the beginning. We needed to be near our damaged home to protect what was left from vandals. After nine months Father Michael asked us to live at an apartment at the church that had come available. Richard was a godsend, he owned a construction company and thanks to him, a year later our home was rebuilt. He helped many others who had damaged or destroyed homes, as well. I've learned in life that the only thing permanent is love of God and our faith. The things of this world are fleeting, indeed.

KEEP YOUR HAND IN HIS!

So, what is next? While life is full of uncertainties, what I do know is that life is also full of surprises and I must trust Jesus above all else. I have gone through joys, sorrows, and many trials of all kinds. I liken trials to riding on a roller coaster, as you travel up the track you put your hand in His. When you hit the peak, you will suddenly fly down with peace and joy to safety!

There have been times in my life when I have felt alone and helpless and I did not know which way to turn. As I look back, I now know that Jesus has never left my side. He has been with me always. He is my constant companion. I talk with him throughout the day no matter where I am or what I am doing. If you have not already, I invite you to fall in love with Jesus and His Church!

Recently, I was asked to speak to a group of young ladies in their teens. They were mostly excited about my adventures in modeling and show business. Many young beautiful stars on television and stage today have mesmerized the younger generation into thinking that being on stage, having fancy clothes, jewels, and other possessions of all kinds is what brings happiness. Real happiness comes by following the ways of Jesus. Staying close to the Catholic Church is the best advice I can give to anyone, at any age, in any profession or in any situation. Having faith is like sleeping peacefully and having sweet dreams despite the ups-and-downs of life.

The greatest day of my life was the day Jesus zapped me with the Holy Spirit when I met Him in the Sacred Heart Church in Atlanta. That day I knew I belonged to Him and to His Church. Since that day I have tried to follow Him in everything I have done, but there are times I have slipped and fallen. He has always helped me to get up!

Our six children are the greatest gifts God gave to Phil and me. Our greatest mission has been to help them return to Him. They are all adults, and there are now eight grandchildren. They are all in church and following the way of Christ. Knowing this, I rejoice, consider it a blessing and I do not take anything for granted but will continue to pray!

Phil lives on with us in our memory and in our hearts. He used to tease me at times when we were visiting friends or family, "Now, don't start talking to everyone. We have to leave." And now, I sometimes look heavenward, and say, "I'm still talking. I'm still sharing my Faith, but I'm coming soon."

Two weeks after Phil left us, I was on a retreat in Venice, Florida. As I walked up to the priest for communion, I asked God, "Phil and I always considered ourselves to be one. Can Phil share my Eucharist whenever I have communion? I was astounded when Father Mallen put two Eucharists in my hand! Later, I asked the priest why he had given me two. "Oh, they just got stuck together," he answered. A few weeks later he was visiting Father Anglim in Fort Myers. I told them the story, and they both howled with laughter. "God does things like that!" he said.

Four years later I was at Cana in the Holy Lands, where Jesus had performed His miracle of changing water to wine at the request of his Holy Mother, Mary. It was April 4, and it just happened to be the anniversary of Phil's death. The priest was blessing marriages of couples that were on the pilgrimage. I expressed a wish to have my marriage with Phil blessed even though he was deceased, and God bless that priest, he honored my wishes and blessed our marriage. Later in the day, as I was walking up to the priest for communion, I asked God, "Is Phil still sharing my Eucharist?" When I was about to receive communion, the priest dropped the Eucharist. I bent down and picked it up. He held up another one. "Take both of them," he said.

Every year those who knew Phil, and those who have come to know him through the Phil Galvano Golf Classic Tournament, remember Phil's legacy—his dedication to helping the youth. My son Peter began the first tournament twenty years ago, as of this writing, in Ft. Myers. Bill and the family, with the Education Foundation in Bradenton have continued the tournament through the years. Today it is one of the most popular golf tournaments in Florida and has raised a lot of money for the Manatee County Education Foundation, benefiting thousands of students in many programs, keeping with Phil's legacy of helping the youth.

Our current pope, Francis Bergolio is a true shepherd. He has inspired me to live simply. I recently downsized from a large home to a two and a half room apartment. At first I was emotional, and some people thought I was out of my mind, but it has brought me true freedom knowing that I cannot hold on to the material things of the past, and it has opened my eyes on where I am heading. Pope Francis and I are the same age. He too decided to live in a two-and-a-half room apartment, instead of the Papal palace.

I want to spend my final days focusing on passing my Catholic faith and my love for His church on to others and this book is part of that mission. I want everyone to be Catholic! I want everyone to know that Jesus loves us so much that He died for us. Whatever I can do or whatever I can say, to inspire everyone to follow Jesus is my heartfelt desire.

Life is like a book. Live each chapter fully, turn the page and live the next chapter and each will add up to make your entire life. Make sure God is the center and the author of your life. You will be delightfully surprised at the ending. Open your hearts! Let Jesus zap you with the Holy Spirit!